THE BOOK OF
SHAMANIC
HEALING

About the Author

Kristin Madden is a homeschooling mom who was raised in a shamanic home. She is the director of Ardantane's School of Shamanic Studies and is a member of the Druid College of Healing. In her spare time, she writes books, works as an environmental chemist, and rehabilitates wild birds.

To Write to the Author

If you wish to contact the author or would like more information about this book, please write to the author in care of Llewellyn Worldwide and we will forward your request. Both the author and publisher appreciate hearing from you and learning of your enjoyment of this book and how it has helped you. Llewellyn Worldwide cannot guarantee that every letter written to the author can be answered, but all will be forwarded. Please write to:

Kristin Madden
⅟ Llewellyn Worldwide
2143 Wooddale Drive, Dept. 0-7387-0271-4
Woodbury, MN 55125-2989, U.S.A.
Please enclose a self-addressed stamped envelope for reply,
or $1.00 to cover costs. If outside U.S.A., enclose
international postal reply coupon.

Many of Llewellyn's authors have websites with additional information and resources. For more information, please visit our website at:
http://www.llewellyn.com

THE BOOK OF
SHAMANIC
HEALING

KRISTIN MADDEN

Llewellyn Publications
Woodbury, Minnesota

First Edition
Third Printing, 2005

Book design and editing by Joanna Willis
Cover design by Kevin R. Brown
Cover image © 2002 by Getty Images
Photos on pages 49–50 © 2002 by WaterHawk Creations

Library of Congress Cataloging-in-Publication Data
Madden, Kristin, 1964–
    The book of shamanic healing / Kristin Madden.—1st ed.
        p.   cm.
    Includes bibliographical references and index.
    ISBN 0-7387-0271-4
        1. Shamanism. 2. Mental healing. I. Title.

    BF1611 .M33 2002
    291.1'44—dc21
                                                            2002016147
ISBN-13: 978-0-7387-0271-1

Llewellyn Publications
A Division of Llewellyn Worldwide, Ltd.
2143 Wooddale Drive, Dept. 0-7387-0271-4
Woodbury, MN 55125-2989, U.S.A.
www.llewellyn.com

 Printed in the United States of America on recycled paper

For my mom,
the most amazing shaman
I've ever met.

CONTENTS

EXERCISES

PREFACE

This book has been in the process of creation for a very long time. In it, I recount some very personal healings of my own. Through writing it, I have delved deeper into my own shadow side than I ever expected. It is not a book that could have been written in a year or two, or even five. This book is the result of decades of growth, learning, pain, and healing. I offer it to you, the reader, in the hope that it will spur you to greater growth and healing in your own life and in your healing work with others.

My shamanic initiations came before I ever heard the word *shamanism*. My maternal grandfather was born in Saamiland (Lapland). He and his family lived a highly spiritual, shamanic lifestyle that was taught to my mother and then me beginning at a very early age. My maternal grandmother was an incredibly psychic woman from the Leeds family of whom Mother Leeds was a well-known wise woman and healer from the east coast of America. It was from these genetic and personal influences that I was introduced to all things shamanic.

My mother has been the family deathwalker for as long as I can remember, in addition to being an incredibly powerful and psychic woman. She was responsible for handling all aspects of the death process for family members and friends. Once these people had passed beyond this reality, they inevitably came to her. Our house was constantly full of Nature spirits and spirits of the dead. It was an amazing way to grow up.

As I got older, my mother taught me much of what she did in a very practical manner. I was included and expected to help. Eventually, upon the arrival of a departed family member, she turned to me and pointedly said, "Someone needs to handle this." From then on, the dead came to me expecting (sometimes demanding) my help. It was pretty much a do-it-or-go-crazy kind of experience and that is exactly how it happened for my mom at around the same age.

My shamanic initiation occurred in a very similar way to my mother's. It came through the death of a grandparent when I was about five years old. While highly psychic and accustomed to out-of-body travel, this opened me up even more to the Otherworlds. Early on, my training came to me through family and directly from the spirits.

Over the years, my mother explored various other mystic paths. I was included in all her explorations. As a result, I got some excellent training in a wide range of healing modalities at a very young age. We practiced and experimented together, combining our abilities for healing, divination, and personal growth. We did a great deal of hands-on and long-distance healing work with both people and animals. Through her influence, I was exposed to both native and modern spiritual paths.

I found myself drawn to healing careers from an early age. When I was in eighth grade, I wanted to be a brain surgeon and had a huge library of books on related topics. I took every first-aid course available and became a lifeguard at a 4-H camp for a few years. Bored with high school, I entered college a year early to get a head start on my career. I could not decide if I wanted to be a biologist or go to medical school, so I entered the premed program and discovered a whole new interest in psychology.

Beyond college, my interests led me to outdoor medicine, wilderness survival, and wildlife rehabilitation. I took graduate courses in environmental chemistry and toxicology as well as wildlife biology. I eventually became a permitted wildlife rehabilitator, focusing a great deal of time on healing wild birds.

During this period of time, I continued spiritual explorations on my own and with my parents. I worked with some native healers and took seminars in some very new methods. I studied druidry with the Order of Bards, Ovates, and Druids, becoming a tutor in time. I worked with a Wiccan coven as a shamanic associate for nearly five years.

I studied and practiced a variety of cultural shamanic paths, including Saami, Tibetan, native North American, and Celtic. I took courses in yoga philosophy and healing at the Himalayan Institute in Pennsylvania. I worked—as I had since childhood—divining for and healing friends and family, but I found that I was also attracting other people in need.

In order to answer this call for healing that kept coming up no matter how busy I kept telling myself I was, I opted to work with specific people outside my family and circle of friends. These were people who were referred to me through word of mouth or who found me in extraordinary ways that felt strongly like spirit guidance.

By this time, I was working with a close-knit group of shamanic practitioners who supported each other in a wide variety of ways. We would bounce ideas off each other and introduce new ideas for experimentation. This was a tremendously productive and creative time for me and I still work with this group at least once a week today.

In the process of working with a growing circle of people in need, I did a great deal of experimenting to determine what methods worked best for what people and what combinations were in effective alignment. I allowed the techniques I had been using for years to change with the specific situation if necessary. I consciously opened to spirit guidance and asked that my ego be set aside so I could function as a channel for the greatest good. I also began to take a new look at ancient methods, particularly my ancestral Celtic and Saami cultures, creating new methods based on traditional wisdom.

Rather than stick solely with the traditionally shamanic techniques I knew, I incorporated hypnosis, kinesiology, neuro-linguistic programming, yoga, pranayama, Reiki and other forms of energy work, homeopathy and flower essences, and more. For diagnosis, I tested the drum, the pendulum, remote viewing, and other methods. Each new phase of testing further refined my own personal "toolkit."

In this book, I offer some information and techniques that are based on indigenous traditions. These are methods that have either been well integrated into modern metaphysical practice, or have been well documented in popular or scholarly literature. I am not divulging anything private or unknown. I offer these ways out of respect for their origins and in the hope that greater healing will be effected through their use.

I want to make it clear that practices such as the vision quest, smudge ceremony, and sweat lodge have their basis in a variety of native cultures from around the world. These are found in the "sitting out" practices in Scandinavia, the sweathouses (*teach an alais*) of the ancient Celts, and the purification by burning herbs in just about every culture. I use these terms because they are commonly understood, but I am not referring to any specific native practice.

There is a surprising amount of similarity among shamanic cultures throughout the world. The use of monotonous sound or ecstatic dance to facilitate altered states of consciousness is one important similarity. The perception of interconnected alternate realities that can be generally broken down into three main worlds is another. The belief that the free soul, or dreaming body, of the shaman leaves the physical body during trance states to travel about this world and the others is a third major similarity.

Each of these commonalities supports the belief that shamans connect with something very real beyond this reality. They speak to the common development of ancient technology to assist in altering brainwave frequencies. These Otherworldly experiences are certainly perceived through cultural symbolism, yet they translate in strikingly similar ways.

Throughout time, shamans have been called upon to serve their communities as healers, oracles, counselors, guides, and deathwalkers.

These are not merely unusual people with bizarre experiences. They are experts in navigating the Otherworlds and returning safely. They are highly functioning and productive members of society with a deep and powerful calling to facilitate the health and harmony of that society.

Shamans are the Wounded Healers and it is this aspect of the shamanic vocation that I will deal with in this book. I make no judgments in these pages as to who is and who is not a true Shaman or who should be called a shamanic practitioner or some other term. Very recently, I have seen the use of the word *shaman* (as opposed to *Shaman*) used much like *druid* is used. While many people may be druids—following a druidic path—a Druid is someone who has attained that grade level as recognized by a specific druidic Order through definite training and initiations. Similarly, a Shaman is a specific role defined and accepted by a particular society, while the shaman is simply someone on the shamanic path.

The point of this book is to assist those that use shamanic methods for healing. My intent is to offer guidance and suggestions so that we may all continue to grow and learn, bringing healing to ourselves and our communities in the process. I am not concerned with what you call yourself here. I am interested in facilitating the benefit to our collective society that may result from your work.

It should be noted that some of the names and specifics described in this book have been altered to protect the privacy of those involved. To see your personal healing and old issues in print can be a great benefit as it reminds you of how far you have come. It can also open old wounds and painfully remind you of where you were.

While this book provides plenty of exercises, suggestions, and charts for your use, I encourage everyone to experiment with these ways and discover what works best for you and for those with whom you are called to enter into a healing partnership. This book is written for the healer, though we can all learn from the information contained in its pages. However, even healers need to continually work on their own personal healing. The path to wholeness and balance does not end once one becomes a Healer. For that reason, many of the exercises and ceremonies in this book are equally as applicable for personal work as they are for work in healing others.

Listen to your intuition and the communication of your spirit guides. All true learning comes from a combination of education and direct experience. Most traditional shamans were predominantly called and trained by the spirits. You will become a better healer when you can put aside your ego and your rational mind and allow your helping spirits to guide your work.

ACKNOWLEDGMENTS

In truth, every being I have met and every experience I have had should be acknowledged for the teacher and opportunity it was. I thank those who supported me and those who did not because each contributed to my own growth and healing in its own way. I truly thank you all for sharing your stories with me and allowing me to retell those stories of which I was a part. I thank you, the reader, for without a reason to write this book, I would not have done such intense work on my own shadows.

My husband and son have truly changed my life. With them, I have become a better person: more complete, more balanced, and more motivated to see myself for who I really am. They have helped me to really love myself, shadows and all. They have also been willing catalysts and "guinea pigs" for my play and experimentation with new methods. Thank you, my best friends. With your love, all things are possible.

My parents are responsible for my wild and crazy upbringing. They teach me with every word and every action to this day. They have been great teachers, parents, and friends, and I feel blessed to have them in my life.

I thank my grandfather, grandmother, and great-aunt for their teachings and support. I honor them for instilling in me a deep respect for my Elders, ancestors, and the natural world. I thank them for showing up in my life long after they were done with their physical bodies.

I thank the members of the current and cyclical Shaman-Circle. Some of you have been my Brothers and Sisters for many years and I honor you. You have all shared stories with me and provided me with a place to share my own stories while I explore new ideas. Heather, West, and Otis were instrumental in helping me find the words I needed to replace the mainstream terms *patient* and *client*.

Those of you who have come to me for healing and have helped me in my own healing deserve my undying gratitude and respect. Those of you who have found benefit in my classes and have shared that with me have given me the greatest of gifts through this sharing. Without you, I would not be who I am today.

Nancy Mostad and Ann Kerns, both at Llewellyn, have been professional and friendly to me since the beginning. It takes a courageous and self-confident person to communicate honestly and quickly no matter what the communication entails. It takes an even stronger person to admit mistakes without defensiveness and to accept apologies with grace. This is an admirable and rare thing to find in any field and I am honored to work with them.

Llewellyn's art department never ceases to impress and amaze me. The publicity department—particularly Lisa Braun and Natalie Harter (who has since moved on to a new position)—have been wonderful and it is a pleasure to work with them. I also want to thank the reviewer of the original manuscript for this book. Your critique and suggestions helped me create a better book.

And last, but certainly not least, I would like to thank Joanna Willis, my editor, for her considerable expertise and willingness to communicate about the editing of this book. I greatly appreciate all your work.

1

WOUNDED HEALERS

While ritual, magicko-spiritual power, and interdimensional journeying are obvious and very significant elements of the shamanic path, woundedness is one of its most vital and least recognized aspects. The shamanic path is one of brutal self-honesty, intense personal healing, and deep self-knowledge. It also includes a responsibility to be of service to one's self and to the community.

The shaman passes through personal wounds, usually beginning with the shamanic initiation, and emerges as a fully transformed being. The new shaman is thereby capable of handling the dangers and responsibilities inherent in the shamanic vocation. This healing and transformation continues for a lifetime. Through this process, the shaman becomes the Wounded Healer.

It is commonly understood that the shamanic initiation often includes the wounding and healing of the shaman by helping spirits. Among traditional shamans, the experience of dismemberment or decapitation is common. This process strips away the original identity of the shaman, removing any association with the body and the current personality.

In facing the spirits of disease and wounding, the new shaman gains complete knowledge of them. Often during these journeys, the spirits will teach the new shaman through the process of reintegration, providing an intimate knowledge of both wounding and healing. In passing through this test of one's complete being, the Wounded becomes Healer.

Many indigenous cultures recreate this aspect of the shaman though their initiation ceremonies, during which the neophyte shaman is ritually killed or wounded. Like all ritual, this serves to ground Otherworldly and profound psychological experience into physical reality. This is also a physical representation of the shamanic initiation by the spirits. These ceremonies may assist members of the community in perceiving the new shaman as a different being than the individual they once knew. The shamanic initiation in the Otherworlds is frequently a psycho-spiritual crisis that manifests as a death-rebirth scenario.

This violent and frightening type of initiation is fairly common, particularly among traditional people. However, it is vital that shamans remain continually open to spirit guidance and work to clear personal issues that may interfere with the work. An initiation alone does not make one a healer or a shaman.

This is an apt description of the shamanic experience. One cannot truly walk this path for any period of time without facing up to one's own wounds. When we consciously open to Otherworldly communication, our spirit guides will not permit us to continue deluding ourselves and avoid personal shadow aspects. Furthermore, our own subconscious selves will project these shadow aspects into our everyday lives and our shamanic journeys.

None of us are completely beyond our personal issues or beliefs. These always have the potential to affect one's judgment and one's ability to heal. This is particularly true if the ego is permitted to get out of control. The need to be right and powerful and knowledgeable can be very effective in putting up blinders and impeding the free flow of energy.

It is also true that our own personal beliefs act as a filter through which we perceive reality. Unless we are aware of these beliefs and how they affect us, the clarity with which we interpret shamanic experience and communications from spirit guides can be compromised. It is a good idea to explore your own personal symbolism and belief systems when developing your shamanic abilities. Self-knowledge is the key to power and protection.

It is especially important to examine those beliefs that appear to be absolute truths.[1] To us, these are not simple beliefs. They are Reality; this is just how the world is/I am. They are easily justified through a variety of means and they are not something we feel is changeable. They are also often not something we feel comfortable exploring.

Absolute truths are dangerous because of our absolute conviction that they are Truth. This doesn't need to be as intense as the existence of a higher power or the presence of gravity. It can be as simple as "The world is a violent place," or "Some people can't be trusted."

We blindly cling to these beliefs. We won't investigate them or where they came from because we don't want to risk losing the security of our reality constructs, even if these constructs make for an often uncomfortable reality. We tell ourselves it is silly to work on these, because they are not just beliefs. In this way, we prevent ourselves from taking the leap to true self-knowledge and freedom. Nothing should be off-limits to our questioning. Resistance within the Self should always be perceived as something to investigate, not avoid.

Often, and particularly early in the path, the frightening images and experiences we encounter during dreaming or in more conscious journeys are our own projections. They are shadow aspects that we have denied. They are searching for a way to be acknowledged, cleared, and integrated. These are opportunities for growth. Unfortunately, we frequently react to these aspects with fear and loathing, slamming yet another door on our inner selves.

---

1. Known as "transparent beliefs" in the Avatar materials.

The individual that has been wounded and healed is most capable of healing—and of understanding the wounds of others. This is especially true when the wounded individual is directly and consciously involved in his or her own healing process. In our own search for wellness and balance, we gain the methods and abilities to heal, and to empower others to create their own healing. This is vital to any path involving service and community.

The empowerment of others is an important point. Shamanic cultures recognize that those in need of healing are an integral and powerful part of the healing team. These individuals must believe and accept the healing in order for the shaman to be most effective. One of many reasons our mechanistic Western medicine is not fully effective, and often does not last when it is effective, is its failure to involve the individual in creating his or her own health.

Health is a different experience than healing. Healing is often defined as curing, fixing, making sound or whole. On the other hand, health is the condition or experience of being whole. Health can also be defined as a sound functional condition. In mainstream Western medicine, health is generally regarded as one's functional condition. Therefore, healing is the remedy for a poor or nonfunctional condition. We get people to the point where they are able to perform in society again. Any greater benefits are incidental, as long as the individual is functioning according to our culture's current standards.

In shamanic societies, a healing is far more than merely restoring physical and mental functioning. A healing involves both shaman and the individual in need. It often includes members of the family or community in a dynamic process of physical, mental, and spiritual cleansing, release, and reintegration. It is understood that health cannot be obtained unless the full being of the person in need is in balance.

Shamans are often called upon because they have passed through the imbalanced and wounded Self and have emerged as balanced, highly functional beings. The shaman knows the roads to healing well after walking them many times in the search for total, integrated health.

In a sense, we are all called to be shamans. We all know how it feels to be wounded; to be sad, hurt, abandoned, angry, confused, and a multitude of other emotions that we would rather not experience. Only through an acceptance and integration of our shadows can we clear our Stuff. Only then can we truly be free. When we allow ourselves the freedom to experience our wounds, we begin the healing process. Yes, this can be painful and difficult, but we are far stronger than we think and we are not alone.

Throughout this book, I examine the various forms of woundedness and their effects on our selves and our communities. Throughout all of this exploration, one thing becomes very clear: we are not alone—and we need not rely on personal power to help us pass through the trials of transformation. The shamanic path brings us experiential evidence of the abundance of supporters, guardians, and guides we have available to us. Shamans possess a heightened awareness of our allies in alternate realities and our interconnections with all of life.

We all have spirit guides, guardian angels, and animal allies. These beings walk with us and assist us in a multitude of ways. This is not the sole realm of the shaman. The shaman is Shaman because of an unavoidable calling that results in tremendous abilities to work with these beings, both in our world and in theirs. However, we all may learn to work with these energies for the benefit of our own spiritual evolution and the continued evolution of our species.

Whether you perceive these energies as archetypal energies, aspects of our own subconscious, or living interdimensional beings is irrelevant. It is your willingness and ability to work with these energies, listen to what they have to teach you, and integrate them into your own Self that is important. As long as it contributes to your personal evolution and the benefit of your society, how you choose to perceive these beings is up to you. To be honest, our limited perception of these energies while we reside in this reality is not fully accurate no matter what we believe them to be.

We experience a representation of the totality of the spirit guide's being. Our perception is certainly increased and expanded through shamanic states of awareness. However, all direct experience must be filtered through consciousness for us to remain aware of it in this reality. What we bring back to consciousness with us is a symbol: something that has passed through the filters of our personal and cultural beliefs and is now accessible to our rational minds.

Through this process we are able to store this experience in our memories and we can then communicate it to others. Our spirit guides rarely exist simply as those mythological beings or animals of this planet that we recognize them as. They manifest to us in ways that are easiest for our conscious minds to handle at any given time. This is why dreams and shamanic journeys are so full of rich symbolism. This is not to say that these beings do not exist independently as specific forms, regardless of our interpretation.

However, this symbolism can be highly personal. Its purpose is to bypass the rational mind in order to speak directly to our spirits. The energy that I experience as Bear has had a huge variety of lessons for me throughout my life. The faces of Bear have changed according to the situation and where I am on my path. But while I best interpret this energy as Bear, it may be very different than the energy that Sue interprets as Bear. It may also be very similar to what Frank interprets as Merlin. In this way, personal symbolism serves to assist us in translating our guides into forms that we can understand and access in this reality.

The road to and through the shadow side is equally symbolic and these symbols are just as personal. We may be presented with dramas and images that have no apparent origin in this reality, yet they are valid and accurate in our particular situations. They are like the binary code that a computer reads. We see no zeros or ones in the graphics and words that show up on our computer screens, but this is how the computer stores them. From these symbols and their specific combinations, my computer knows that I am writing these words and not playing a computer game. When I access this file tomorrow, I will read this chapter and not see my son's computer game.

Our brains function as living holographic computers and play a significant role in the body/mind/spirit connection. It is in the brain that interdimensional communication and experience is translated into the symbols of language and the images of this reality. The brain is the major storage facility for memory and personal symbolism, and functions as a type of stabilizing guidepost for the shamanic traveler.

When we experience contact with alternate realities, this experience is funneled through the brain where it is compared to everything else in our memory banks. In general, any experience or image that does not resemble anything previously experienced is discarded. This is one reason why many of us fail to remember our dreams: they do not easily translate into any known symbols.

Those experiences that bear a similarity to something in our memories are interpreted according to what we already understand. For example, the spirit woman of light that met me during a shamanic journey and informed me that I was pregnant was not a real human woman and it is doubtful that she chooses to take that form all the time. Yet this was the type of energy I recognized in this being. It was also the best form for me to receive her message in at that time.

It is interesting to note that this particular part of that journey was not immediately accessible to my conscious mind. Although I easily recalled every other part of the journey, there was a blank spot at one level of the Upperworld. I knew something significant had happened, but my rational mind needed more time to process this experience. Several hours later, I spontaneously remembered everything. It was as though my brain had completed its translation and it was released to my consciousness in one huge flood of memory. It came through so fast that I had difficulty writing it down quickly enough.

Shadow aspects and wounds are stored throughout the body, often in the form of symbols. They are like computer viruses that are hidden within a loop of larger, active files. These viruses are not readily apparent to us. We may have to really search for them, yet they still have the power to dramatically impact our reality. If left unchecked and uncleared, they can wreak havoc on our systems.

Shadow aspects work in similar ways. Our day-to-day habits and patterns are the larger, active files. These are the visible elements of our realities. We look for most of our cause and effect here in the obvious. While there usually is a direct relationship between our physical actions and the consequences, this is not always the case. Even more often, the reasons for our physical actions and emotional responses are frequently not clear.

It is difficult to heal an unseen wound or cure an illness when we don't know what is causing the symptoms. Healing one's psycho-spiritual wounds is made more difficult because we, as ego-identities, are afraid to give up control of the consciousness. The ego fears dissolution and has taken on the responsibility of preventing pain and vulnerability, as well as preventing access to the deeper regions of the Self.

The ego does not want to let go of the power in this incarnation and so it mistakenly fears its own death in confronting our shadows. What the ego is unable to see is that big picture. While it is true that reintegration of shadow aspects can be painful and the ego will not be the same once this is accomplished, the ego does not die off. It evolves with the rest of one's being and becomes a more expanded part of the Self. No longer does the ego continually need to reassert itself in the face of potential threats. Suddenly, we are secure in our own existence and in our interconnections with all of life. We find that differences of opinion are nothing more than varying perspectives of beings that currently occupy different places on the path of evolution. We are comfortable in accepting and even learning from those differences.

This is the best healing that the shamanic path can bring to us as individuals and as a society. The only real differences between us are our perspectives and our beliefs. Therefore war, violence, and religious conversion are truly irrelevant wastes of time. Reality is subjective and is based on our beliefs. Through the direct experience of spirit guides, alternate realities, and the lands of the dead, we gain a significantly expanded perspective. The issues of this reality become far less personal when we realize that our "person" is far more than this personality.

In other words, your point of view is your point of view and it has no bearing on my spiritual path. I am here in this body at this time to take care of my own stuff and to work on my own spiritual development. Only I can walk my path and I cannot walk yours for you. I cannot possibly know what experiences and beliefs are necessary for your soul at this time. Beyond all our beliefs, we are One; interconnected and more divine than we realize. Therefore, judgment is pointless. The only honest and wise choice is to accept each being and each experience as a potential teacher and learn what we can.

That certainly is easier said than done. It is also a simple thing to recognize what others need to learn; much simpler than realizing what our own lessons are. It is much more comfortable to let the issues slide and deal with them another time or in another lifetime. That is what reincarnation is for, isn't it? Why do those on the shamanic path put themselves through so much in one lifetime?

There are as many reasons for this as there are those walking a shamanic path. However, in most instances it is an inevitable side effect of the shamanic Calling. On some level we have decided, along with our guides, that we will not be permitted to ride it out this time around. Our guides may need to assume the role of "bad guy," forcing us to see and experience difficult things for our own spiritual growth. This begins with the shamanic initiation and continues throughout the life of the shaman.

At one point, I was resting easy. I was delighting in the wonderful new creations we had accomplished and, frankly, was getting lazy. Life was good and I wanted to enjoy that for as long as possible. I was happy and I wanted to avoid facing those remaining shadow aspects that I knew were still present. That is a wonderful place to be, but it cannot last forever. To try to halt everything at one happy place is not only fruitless, but it denies the trust we have in Spirit and attempts to dishonor ourselves by pausing evolution.

My guides were not about to let me get away with that. They made it painfully clear that I needed to get off my butt and start doing some serious shamanic work. During a journey to scope out one specific shadow aspect, I was pulled into the constellation Great Bear. Bear pulled me in and held me in her heart, then sat me down for a talk.

I asked how to clear this aspect that I perceived as negative. Bear said, "You don't," and smacked me once on each cheek. With tears of pain, I touched each cheek to find blood and skin ripped by open claws. Bear placed a necklace of bear fur and claws around my neck and told me, among other things, to ". . . stop judging it and use it. . . . You have opened the way; you must work with it!"

When the journey ended, I looked in the mirror, half expecting to see my face shredded and bloody. I knew with absolute certainty that another journey lay ahead of me in this reality and that it was time to get back on the path.

This is not to say that the shamanic initiation and our interactions with spirit guidance are only about facing difficulties and mortality. It can be a lot of fun, but it is most definitely always enlightening. The shamanic initiation manifests in many forms. The classical death, dis- memberment, and ingestion scenario is not necessarily the most common. Sometimes we do need to be kicked in the teeth for us to wake up and take notice. However, there are those for whom this is unnecessary and would be counterproductive.

Many people experience varying degrees of merging with spirit guidance, or shapeshifting. This is a gentler method of initiation, but is no less powerful. Shapeshifting can take years of work to accomplish consciously. When part of an initiatory experience, it is a good indication that the shaman-to-be is open and accepting of the Calling, as well as relatively clear of limiting beliefs. This does not necessarily mean the individual does not have significant work ahead of him or her, but things may go a bit more smoothly without a huge burden of blocks.

This decision to "take it all on" is also a side effect of shamanic practice. One cannot walk the roads of the Otherworlds and be called as Healer without the impact of these blocks and conditions becoming crystal clear. We know from direct experience that healing and passing into the next world is made much easier when one's personal wounds are handled early on. As I describe in *Shamanic Guide to Death and Dying,* these experiences and beliefs are re-experienced at the moment of death.[2] These uncleared issues are also part of the after-life review with spirit guides, and they will be repeated in another incarnation until they are properly handled.

A good friend once reminded me of the interesting cliché, "That which does not kill us, makes us stronger." People often say this in the midst of a crisis or tragedy. Rarely does it seem to hold much healing or truth for them. It often comes across as a platitude, something we tell people to try to make them feel better about the fact that the world has just come crashing down on their heads. "Yeah, yeah, yeah . . . whatever . . ." We don't believe it is true and we don't really want to hear it from other people.

---

2. Madden, *Shamanic Guide,* 112.

Like many of our societal clichés, this one contains a good deal of truth and bears further exploration. When we are able to face up to life's challenges and traumas and move through them without losing ourselves in the process, we necessarily become stronger beings. No longer can we hide and say, "I can't . . ." We know that we can.

These situations change us. Ideally, we grow through these challenges as we meet them and pass through them. Often, it is the ability to trust and experience one's own vulnerability that defines one's strength. Certainly, these experiences allow us more understanding into specific situations.

Unfortunately, many of us do not emerge whole. Although we may have tackled the challenge and we may have done what needed to be done, a great many of us suffer varying degrees of wounding in the process. Often, these wounds remain with us for years because we wall them off while they are still raw and allow them no light or air or anything they may need to heal.

Most of the time, this is the only way we can get through these experiences. We are protecting the Self in the only way possible at the time. This is beneficial in that it allows the identity to move forward; it sacrifices certain aspects to preserve the individual.

Sometimes we are able to face these wounds again. Through therapy or spontaneous memories, we can re-experience the wound and its cause. Yet, if we are not prepared to release the pain and accept the experience, no healing will occur. In fact, hypnosis or soul retrievals that are performed before the individual is ready for reintegration can be even more traumatic and cause further wounding. Furthermore, if the belief or cause of the repression has not been cleared, a long-term healing will not be possible.

We must do more than just relive these painful experiences. We need to prepare for this process by doing a considerable amount of personal shamanic work. Certainly this does not need to be done within a shamanic framework, but this is my path and my main means of describing the process. We work with our spirit guides to help clear out the easy stuff. We use journeying, dreaming, storytelling, and more to get on to the path of self-knowledge. This preliminary work must be done before we can hope to effect long-term healing for anyone.

I have seen and read about shamanic healings and soul retrievals that initially seemed to be beneficial. The clients experienced an emotional release and left feeling very hopeful. Unfortunately, many of these people experienced a recurrence of the same situations or found that within a few months of the session nothing had changed. These people often end up feeling betrayed or let down. Some decide that they or their problems just can't be fixed and sink deeper into destructive patterns.

This is one reason for the importance I place in this book on preparing for healing—both for the individual in need and the healer. First and foremost, we must choose to do no harm to ourselves or to others. All the best intentions will be pointless if we push ahead in an attempt to help another person or gain healing for ourselves and create more wounding.

Before choosing to offer any form of healing, healers must work to heal themselves. They must have cleared a significant amount of their own shadows in order to recognize and understand the necessary healing methods. We go into healing for two reasons: because we have a spiritual mandate to do so, and to be of service to those in need.

Healing from within one's ego is rarely fully effective and can be detrimental to all concerned. When individuals in need come to us for assistance, it is our responsibility to do what it takes to heal them or to refuse to take on the case. To heal takes the ability to be open to spirit guidance; to step beyond our identities and allow universal Medicine to flow through us.

By this, I do not mean to say that only those that have fully healed and worked through all the big stuff should act as healers. I would never discourage anyone from following their hearts in this. My main point is to highlight the fact that this is an ongoing process. Healers work on healing themselves for their entire lives. My other main goal is to point out that we each need to be mindful of possible alternate interpretations for what we see, and watch for our own projections in those that come to us for healing.

The power to heal comes not from within this body or the identity of this particular incarnation, but from the Great Spirit, the God and Goddess, or from whatever name you choose to give the divine Source of All Life. To rely on one's own personal power only depletes our own energy, leaves us open to imbalances, and detracts from the full flow of healing energy that should be received by the person in need. Effective healing makes full use of the spirit guides of all involved.

This is vital to the healing process. When we deal with someone else's wounds in an empathetic way, whether psychically or shamanically, we allow our energy fields to be open to them. Ceasing or postponing personal work and communication with spirit guides increases the possibility that we will hold some of that wounding. While we work with grounding energy, we may not clear everything, particularly when a person in need is mirroring something within us that we have not yet dealt with—one of our own shadows. Our guides will know instantly and can alert us to the need for additional work on ourselves if we allow them to and ask for their help.

When we become caught up in the ego and this personality, we permit ourselves to move back into wounding. We also block effective communication from spirit guides. Our perception in all realities becomes limited and we may find ourselves stuck in beliefs and transitory desires once again. At this point, we have strayed off the path of the shaman. Our shadows gain control and we find conflict and pain where we once found opportunity and growth. Where once we recognized the reasons for certain situations, we now only rail at the injustice of life.

The path of the Wounded Healer is not easy. It is a lifelong process that has its ups and downs and may cycle back around just to ensure that an issue is fully clear. In spite of the difficulty of this path, the benefits of walking it are beyond compare. They carry over into the next world, and the next life if we have one. More than that, it is always an adventure.

2

PREPARING TO HEAL

Many people are natural healers. They were born with easy access to healing abilities and often appear to intuitively channel the most beneficial energy for someone in need. Most of us are acquainted with someone that just knows how to make other people feel better without even intending to "heal." Yet, even these people need to learn to be Healers if they are to work most effectively for those that come to them for healing assistance.

Any form of healing requires training and experience. Shamanic healing is no different. It involves much more than traveling out of body, sending energy, or creating elaborate rituals. It demands that a healer-to-be study shamanic techniques and delve deeply into personal shadows.

Certainly modern shamanism is dynamic. There is plenty of opportunity to create or alter techniques, provided you are not working within a traditional path. However, in order to do so, a healer must have clear and open communication with spirit guides, as well as a solid basis of understanding in time-honored techniques.

Traditionally, a new shaman might have the benefit of an association with experienced shamans of the same community. The neophyte would often have an initiatory ritual and some degree of training with these elder shamans. Yet even in most of these cultures, it was recognized that true learning came from the spirits themselves—and through experience.

Today, we have a great many philosophies and techniques available to us. We have fairly easy access to cultural information from around the world. Books on a wide variety of scientific and metaphysical theories abound. We can take classes in just about every healing method known to humankind. We can even get certification in most of these methods, but neither certification nor the collection of knowledge can make one a Healer. That comes from a balance between learning and intuition, knowledge and wisdom, and from both spirit guides and experience.

With this balance between intuition and knowledge in mind, we can proceed with a discussion on the learning that can contribute to the healing vocation. In *Hands of Light,* Barbara Brennan makes some very specific recommendations for training that, in her belief, healers must have to be effective. She believes in a great deal of technical training, such as anatomy and physiology, psychology, pathology, and alternative healing methods. She writes that a healer "must have some knowledge of these methods to understand how they dovetail to make a healing a whole one, and to be able to communicate with the other people involved in the case."[1]

A degree of mainstream and technical knowledge can be beneficial, even for the healer who was raised in a shamanic family and works only with close family members. When and if someone comes to you with a serious condition, it can be essential to be able to interpret your findings in terms of the physical body or emotional state and communicate them to a mainstream medical professional if necessary. This is particularly important when it comes to physical issues, such as tumors, disease, injuries, and so on.

---

1. Brennan, *Hands of Light,* 13.

However, I must point out that this is not necessary for everyone. A formal or extensive training in any of these fields is not required unless you plan to become a professional healer and work with healing teams involving mainstream medical personnel. There are plenty of healers who limit their work to one specific area, such as energy work or herbal remedies. While it is true that continuing education increases one's effectiveness, a college course in anatomy is not necessarily required for the healer specializing in soul retrieval.

A less formal training is often all the healer needs. This may take the form of reading manuals and journals or taking short seminars in anatomy and psychology. It may be an apprenticeship with a folk healer or it may simply be the result of one's own experience with family members. Education may take many forms. What we deem necessary is based on our interest and on the level of healing we intend to practice.

Some healers seem to channel just the right words whenever they are counseling people. When they relax and allow Spirit to guide their words and actions, they communicate effectively and truly connect with people on a deep level. I find that when I relax and release my attachment to the identities of all involved, I can more easily feel the other person and my spirit guides will often speak directly through me. This is a gift that should be encouraged and supported.

It is important to avoid becoming overly intellectual or allowing the ego to create a need to be right all the time. This can block the intuitive flow. As a result, communications become too logical and thought-driven. These healers may lose access to this innate ability to connect with people in need. Again, my point is that we need to find a healthy balance.

Personal Preparation

Mainstream medical doctors enter examination rooms every day without any more preparation than reading a chart or glancing at the complaint. They enter these rooms carrying with them all the stresses of the day and all their personal feelings. They are also quite possibly carrying trace energies from all their previous patients. Through all of this, they most often use logic or mental guesswork to determine the illness and the "cure."

Shamanic healers are very conscious of the effect their personal energy can have on another person, particularly one that is already vulnerable. It would be irresponsible and potentially damaging for a healer to bring personal issues and the energies of prior healing sessions into the space of a person in need. The shamanic healer recognizes that it is not possible to function as a truly clear channel through all this extra stuff.

Personal stresses and preoccupation with another case may impair or even block communication with spirit guides. It would be easy for a healer to miss something or project something on to the situation at hand in this state. Therefore, it is essential that we continue with our personal shamanic work on an ongoing basis. It is equally important to prepare for each healing session.

Many healers find that some form of physical exercise is the best way to begin a day of healing. Personally, I find that exercise releases tension and allows me to more easily enter trance. My body is more relaxed and I find that I am automatically more open to spirit guidance. This does not need to be a five-mile run for it to be effective.

One of the most beneficial movement meditations I have learned is a series of exercises that a friend taught my mother and me to use as preparation for more advanced yoga. I have altered it slightly to create a movement meditation that I use specifically to get my energy flowing for healing. This may be performed sitting or standing, and before or after the EarthStar meditation outlined below. It is also simple enough to be done periodically throughout a day filled with healing sessions.

PREPARATORY MOVEMENT MEDITATION

Begin with three deep breaths. Breathe deeply into your diaphragm, filling your lungs. Feel your ribs, chest, and shoulders expand, and release. If you feel any tension, breathe into these areas and allow the breath to expand and release the tension.

Drop your head to your chest. Allow the tension to release from your neck and release your breath. Now, moving counterclockwise, slowly bring your ear to your shoulder as you inhale. Allow your head to fall backward, then sink to the other shoulder on the exhalation. Feel your neck stretch in all directions without pushing it. Complete three full circles, and switch directions to complete three more circles in the clockwise direction. Permit your mind to go blank.

Stand or sit tall and straight. Take note of how your body feels. Be aware of any feelings or thoughts that come up. Acknowledge them without judgment and release them.

Raise your shoulders as high as you can. On the inhalation, squeeze your shoulders blades together and circle your shoulders to the back. Feel your chest open. On the exhalation, bring your shoulders down, then together in front of you. Feel your back expand. Repeat this three times in each direction.

Stand or sit tall and straight. Take note of how your body feels. Be aware of any feelings or thoughts that come up. Acknowledge them without judgment and release them.

Continue the same process by circling your wrists, your legs at the hips, and your feet at the ankles.* Stop in between each step to observe your body and mind.

---

*If possible, a person sitting down should raise each leg to circle the entire leg at the hip joint. This need not be a large circle, just enough to provide some motion in the joint. If at any time you experience pain or are unable to move a joint, skip that step and move on.

An essential preparation for healing is the clearing and purification of our personal energy fields. This is possibly one of the most important aspects of healing to keep in mind when working for more than one person in a day. When we are clear and centered, all else tends to flow easily. For many people, the smudge or drum purification ceremonies in chapter 6 are ideal for this. Other people prefer a guided visualization, sitting in silence for a time, or a moving meditation. The EarthStar meditation is excellent for this purpose. It is a general clearing, and countless people have used variations on the same theme over the years.

EARTHSTAR MEDITATION

Calm and center yourself. Count yourself down from ten to one. It may help to visualize yourself going down one step with each descending number. Remember to take deep, diaphragmatic breaths and feel yourself going deeper.

See a ball of light at the center of the Earth. This is the embodiment of Earth energy. See this energy flow up out of the Earth's core and into your body through the soles of your feet and the base of your spine. If you like, place your hands, palms down, on the ground and allow this energy to be drawn directly up into your hands and arms. Feel this energy fill your entire body. Feel it pour out from the pores of your skin, your eyes, your hair, your navel. Feel it flow completely though you and out through the top of your head. Fully experience this flow.

See a star at the center of the universe. This is the embodiment of the universal or Sky energy. See this energy flow down from the center of the star and into your body through the top of your head. If you like, raise your hands, palms up, to the sky and allow this energy to be drawn directly down into your hands and arms. Feel this energy fill your entire body. Feel it pour out from the pores of your skin, your eyes, your hair, your navel. Feel it flow completely though you and down into the Earth. Fully experience this flow.

Experience both of these flows together for as long as you like, until you really feel them. See and feel your total energy space cleansed and purified by this light.

Visualize yourself completely attuned to your higher Self. See yourself acting as a clear channel for healing energy. You are revitalized by these energies flowing through your being.

You may now choose whether to count yourself back up from one to ten or not. In any case, you are now ready to enter the space of a vulnerable individual. One note of advice: maintain this energy flow while you are with this person. If you begin to feel drained or irritable, take a moment alone to call forth this flow. As long as this energy is flowing through you, you are protected from any draining or damaging energies.

The following exercise is very effective when used immediately after the previous one, allowing the energy flow of EarthStar to naturally progress into the visualization below. The main goal of the Necklace of Lights meditation is to restore energy flow while balancing the specific chakras. However, it is also effective in clearing and balancing the total energy field. I offer both for your experimentation. You may choose to use one without the other or reverse the order. Only you can decide what meditations and exercises to include in your personal toolkit, and these may vary with the day or the situation at hand.

NECKLACE OF LIGHTS MEDITATION

See and feel your total energy space cleansed and purified by light. Your body appears to be a long cord of white light.

Now see a ball of violet light coming from the top of your head. It is like a purple bead on your cord of light.

Feel and see this beautiful violet energy. Stay with this ball of light until you fully experience it.

At the center of your forehead is deep, dark blue ball of light; another bead on the necklace that is you. Feel and see this beautiful, deep, dark blue energy. Stay with this ball of light until you fully experience it.

In the middle of your throat is a ball of bright blue energy. Feel and see this beautiful bright blue energy. Stay with this ball of light until you fully experience it.

In the center of your chest, right by your heart, is a beautiful ball of green energy. Feel and see this beautiful green energy. Stay with this ball of light until you fully experience it.

Move your attention down to the ball of golden energy at your solar plexus. Feel and see this beautiful golden yellow energy. Stay with this ball of light until you fully experience it.

In the middle of your abdomen, see a ball of vibrant orange energy. Feel and see this beautiful orange energy. Stay with this ball of light until you fully experience it.

At the base of your spine is a deep red ball of energy. Feel and see this beautiful red energy. Stay with this ball of light until you fully experience it.

See these balls of energy on the cord of white light that is your body, like beads on a white necklace. Feel how it feels to be fully relaxed and balanced. Know that you can feel this way any time you want to, just by remembering the feeling of this necklace.

Once the personal energy field is clear, we call in spirit guidance. You may choose to do this from the peaceful state of the above meditations, or hold a full ceremony. Whatever feels right and is appropriate for the space and situation is fine. It may or may not be acceptable to you and the individual you are working with to enact a full pagan circle casting or drumming and smudging between each session or in a hospital.

Normally it is sufficient to call upon your spirit guides and ask for their blessings in the work you are about to do. Your usual guides may be in attendance at all sessions or you may find that a specific guide for healing comes through at these times. Be aware of any unusual changes in the guides you perceive at a healing session. You may want to ask newcomers if they are there for you. You may be connecting with the spirit guides of the person in need. It is also possible for an incoming entity to be specifically associated with the particular complaint or illness.

Preparing the Room

The next step includes the creation of sacred space. To create a sacred space is to set aside your working area, outside of everyday time and space. This creates a psychic barrier to any energies that might distract or impair your healing session. Sacred space is purified, consecrated, and protected. Not only does this assist you in attaining the necessary healing and intuitive frame of mind, but it also facilitates feelings of safety and harmony in those that come to you for assistance, particularly those that are psychically sensitive.

If you are working as a healer, even only within your family, you may already have a special room for this work. This should be a room that is dedicated to this type of work. Limiting its use to healing work, if at all possible, will guard the energy here. If you do have a dedicated space for this work, you will want to make decoration choices with the assistance of your spirit guides. Soothing and inviting colors and fabrics help create a feeling of safety and comfort.

The working space should be clean and free of clutter. If possible, replace your fluorescent lights with full-spectrum ones. Make sure your room has at least one box of tissues. Living plants are a wonderful addition to any healing space for their ability to cleanse the air and to bring in that living earth energy. You might also want to have water or tea and some soothing music available. The space should be decorated in a way that makes it feel inviting and comfortable but is light and organized.

You may have a specific pouch—perhaps a Crane Bag or Medicine pouch—for healing work that has a place of honor in the room. Special crystals or other stones and sacred artwork may be placed accordingly. These crystals and stones are a wonderful way of collecting excess energy that is released during a healing session. They can then be purified afterward and charged with healing energy.

The following exercise may be used to charge crystals, jewelry, and even entire rooms with healing energy. When used to charge one's personal space or the room itself, it can be the first step in creating sacred space. Crystals in particular have a way of amplifying and projecting the energy we put into them.

CHARGING ITEMS WITH ENERGY

Clear your energy field using any of the meditations described above or purification ceremonies outlined in chapter 6.

Place your hands on or over the items you have selected for charging. If you have chosen an entire room, or something you are unable to place your hands over, hold out your hands with your palms facing the item. Feel this energy you have cleared and merged with flow through you and out the palms of your hands. See the item completely cleared of any previous energies. Say aloud or to yourself, "May this _____ be purified and cleared of all unwanted energies and beings."

Call upon your guides, God, or the Source of All Life, and ask that you be used as the channel to fill this object/room with pure healing energy. As you direct this energy, see those who will be coming in for healing feeling safe and comforted in this energy. Clearly visualize the healing and unconditional love that is filling this object.

When you feel ready, lower your hands. It may help to rub them together to speed the desensitization. Many healers can experience overly sensitized hands and feet, often resulting in extreme heat, tingling, or numbness.

Give thanks to those you invoked and to all who assisted you in this process before returning to ordinary reality.

The general metaphysical view of the semipermeable circle or sphere is possibly the easiest way to visualize sacred space. It is reminiscent of the auric egg that surrounds each of us on certain layers of the personal energy field. We can visualize it as a glowing sphere of protection that holds a meditative and beneficial energy inside while it guards us from outside influences.

When we create sacred space for a healing session, we allow protective and healing energy to flow through us and out around the room in a sphere, completely surrounding everything in the room. This is generally sealed with a request that spirit guides or the Great Spirit maintain this sphere of energy. The healer asks that only the most beneficial energies be allowed to pass into the sphere but that all unwanted energies be immediately released from within this space.

Not all cultures or individuals actually create or cast a circle, although the circle is an important concept in most aboriginal cultures. Celtic shamans may call upon the Realms of Earth, Sky, and Sea to surround and protect the working space. Shamans of other cultures may call upon the Spiritkeepers of the Four Directions for protection and guidance.

In these ways, the energy of the working space is often purified first through the use of burning herbs or the use of sound, such as bells, rattles, or drums. Then the spirits of the land and sky are invited and asked for their blessings and protection. The energetic and psychological effects are the same as in casting a circle.

CREATING SACRED SPACE

Purify the area using the smudge or drum purification ceremony in chapter 6.

Place an offering to the Spirits of Place in the center of the area. Take a deep breath. As you release it, breathe out a prayer of thanks for these spirits and their blessings. Let them know that you honor them with this gift.

Beginning at North or East (whichever feels most correct to you), invite the Spiritkeepers of the Four Directions to join you in this sacred space. Ask for their blessings on this work you are about to do. Request their protection from any unwanted energies and let them know you are open to their guidance.

Coming to Center, invite the Sky Father and Earth Mother to join you in this sacred space. Ask for their blessings on this work you are about to do. Request their protection from any unwanted energies and let them know you are open to their guidance.

Finally, ask for the guidance and protection of the Great Spirit or Creator, who is always present in all things. Allow yourself to be open to any communication from this Source.

Take a moment to feel these energies surrounding your work area. Trust that you are protected and blessed in this sacred space. Give thanks to all for their presence.

CLOSING SACRED SPACE

Thank the Spirits of Place for their blessings and protection. Honor their presence and their roles as Keepers of this place.

Beginning at North or East (whichever feels most correct for you), thank the Spiritkeepers of the Four Directions for their protection and blessings. If you received special guidance from any of them, acknowledge and honor this gift. Thank them for their continued blessings throughout your life and ask that your every action might honor them.

Coming to Center, thank the Sky Father and Earth Mother for their protection and blessings. If you received special guidance from them, acknowledge and honor this gift. Thank them for their continued blessings throughout your life and ask that your every action might honor them.

Finally, thank the Great Spirit or Creator for being with you every step of the way and for all the blessings you receive each day. Take a moment to be still and open to any communication from this Source.

Meeting and Greeting

We greet people in need of healing from within the sanctified energy of sacred space. When they arrive, they are met with a calm and inviting energy that permeates the healing space and emanates from within us. As the healer, it is your responsibility to ensure that everyone coming to you is greeted lovingly, yet appropriately.

If you are primarily working with family members, your manner will obviously be more familiar than with other people. This is particularly true with immediate family members, such as lovers and children. However, a confident and professional demeanor is important even with family. This instills a sense of faith and trust in your abilities. This alone will contribute to healing, because they believe in you as Healer.

When meeting with people outside your family, it is important to find a balance between being gently welcoming and being professional. You do not want to re-create the authoritarian and sterile atmosphere of a medical doctor's office, but you don't want it to be excessively casual either, especially if there is to be a monetary transaction.

True professionals are businesslike without being curt or cold. They take charge of a healing session by informing the individual in advance of what form the session will take, what might occur, and what is expected of this individual as healing partner. These types of healers take notes of all the facts and symptoms as specifically and clearly as possible. They record any dreams, experiences, memories, or life situations that might be relevant. They do not make extraordinary promises and they are as honest as possible without causing harm.

Professional healers are interested and caring yet they do not allow themselves to get caught up in emotional dramas. This does not contribute to healing and is likely to be counterproductive. If a person does not want healing but prefers to continue to create the situation and feed off the drama, that is their choice. As healers we do not benefit anyone if we get involved and provide more energy to this type of situation. We simply let them know that we will be available when they are ready to co-create their own healing.

If you come across anything that makes you uncomfortable or afraid in a meeting or healing session, have an emergency plan already in place. You should not be working in an area where you are completely alone and cannot reasonably expect someone to hear you yell or pound on a wall. If something develops that you cannot handle, have a list of emergency contacts to call. These should include the police, ambulance, psychiatrist or psychologist, another healer, and anyone else that might be able to assist with difficult problems.

The potential for personal danger or an emergency situation is very low. However, it can exist and this is one important reason to get as much training as possible before going into practice. It is much more likely that situations that make you uncomfortable will involve intense reactions on the part of those you are healing. It is essential that the healer neither overreact nor attempt to handle a potentially dangerous situation alone.

For example, I worked with one gentleman who would hyperventilate whenever we got close to a target issue. I could have pushed harder to force him to face these issues. I could have stopped and called an ambulance out of fear that he would black out or was having a heart attack. Both of these would have created real problems for both of us. I did neither of these things. We proceeded gently by incorporating other techniques, and everything worked out quite well.

Below I offer a basic checklist that you may use as a reference when starting out. It is also valuable in reviewing your current practices to see if anything has been overlooked. Please feel free to add to and alter this as you see fit.

Checklist: Creating a Professional Healing Experience

1. Have room prepared and necessary tools or journal ready.

2. Be personally prepared to focus on the healing at hand.

3. Have sacred space created.

4. Dress comfortably, yet not in a manner that might be intimidating (i.e., highly costumed or sexual).

5. Greet people with confidence and care but without overt emotion or excessive touching.

6. Handle any monetary or bartering transactions before getting started.

7. Explain your background and style. Ensure that the person in need has a basic understanding of the terms you will use. Stress the concept of partnership in healing.

8. Ask questions and engage in discussion in a friendly, nonjudgmental manner. Do not get involved in emotional outbursts. Take notes to ensure an accurate memory of what was discussed and what occurred.

9. If anything makes you personally uncomfortable or afraid, politely but firmly ask the person to leave. Have safety measures in place in the event of an emergency.

10. Describe what you plan to do and ask permission for any physical contact.

11. Be very clear about anything you want the individual to do or focus on.

12. Ground the energy after a session and ensure the person is ready to leave on his or her own if an escort is not available.

13. Take final notes and hold a debriefing discussion after the session. Inform the individual of any messages you received. Describe any "homework" you want him or her to do and make plans for any follow-ups that are needed.

14. Thank the person for participating in this session and for working toward his or her own healing. Say good-bye in the same professional manner you greeted this person.

15. Clear the room and your energy before moving on to another session.

16. Continue to work on your own self-knowledge and the development of your healing skills.

Because of the recent popularity of shamanic techniques and their impact on the psyche, it can be difficult for a person seeking healing to know the experienced and ethical healers from the rest. This uncertainty impacts both potential "clients" and healers. In the hopes of avoiding much of the potential grief that can result from this situation, I recommend that healers make up a checklist or create a Partnership Brochure for new people.

The Partnership Brochure is something tangible that people can take home from an initial meeting or healing session. The points included in it should all have been covered in the preliminary discussions, but it is often helpful for the individual to have something to look at when there is some time to reflect. The Partnership Brochure might include a healer's biography, including information on your training and experience. State that references are available upon request and be prepared to offer them if asked. The brochure will also include an overview of the shamanic process and the importance of an active partnership.

Holding these discussions (see number 7 in above checklist) from the very beginning will save both of you a lot of grief later on. The healer will not be held up to a potentially impossible standard of perfection. The person in need of healing will be empowered to begin creating the life experience they want. There will be no blame or resentment if the case requires a different method, takes longer than was hoped, or if the individual seeking healing refuses to participate or blocks the healing process. Sometimes they truly are not yet ready and we cannot force the process.

Payment

In ancient times, healers and shamans did not accept monetary payment for their services. They lived in a culture that supported their work and some form of payment was always forthcoming. Many of the modern shamanic healers I know still refuse money for their services, preferring a form of barter system in which goods or services are exchanged. Sometimes there is simply a promise to help and return the favor when it is most needed.

There are those who have devoted their lives to this work and need to charge money for it. We no longer live in a society that supports the full-time work of shamanic healers. These people should not be denigrated for charging a fee. This is simply another form of energy exchange. For them to devote their lives to this type of work is a gift to all of us. They deserve to live comfortable lives just the like the rest of us.

Unfortunately, money comes with a great deal of psychological baggage in modern society. When we pay for something, we demand to get our money's worth. We expect success and we may feel we are in a position of control over the services offered. We weigh whether or not the service is worth the sum we are paying and if this is in keeping with the "market." This puts a great deal of pressure on the process and the healer.

Money also has the potential to directly influence the healer. Most people today demand an annual raise in their jobs. They are working toward something better: a promotion, a bigger house, a new boat.

More money is needed to do these things and we feel we really deserve that if we are good at our jobs. While healing is not like most other "jobs," this dynamic is likely to arise.

I know that when I was a chemist, it was important for me to keep moving up in terms of salary. I would move on to a new company or a new position and get an increase, but somehow the money was never enough. I felt the stress and the hours deserved more and more until my main focus was money. I was miserable and the career lost most of its appeal for me as a result. For a healer to lose that passion is a dangerous thing for all involved.

I also feel that, in certain situations, a monetary fee makes it very easy on the person in need. They are able to spend some money and forget about it. They have not invested any time or energy in this and, therefore, they have no real responsibility for the success of the process.

I once worked with a man who had worked with most of the "shamans" in my area. He was dealing with a difficult situation and had given up his personal power. Each of these practitioners charged him a hefty fee and promised to fix his problem. They did the hour or two of their particular methods and left. In order to get more assistance, he had to pay more money. When nothing changed, he was left feeling that his problem was insurmountable and things got worse.

I refused to allow this man to give me a donation for the work I did, but I demanded that he begin to work for himself in a variety of ways. My working group and I provided energetic and psychological support and protection throughout the process. I gave him the exercises and meditations he needed to do and I worked with him in person. I told him that he might experience a spontaneous change, but it might also take some time to feel the effects of our work.

His entire attitude changed for the better when I refused his money. He agreed to do the work himself when he realized that we would be supporting him energetically. It took about a month before he began to feel lighter. That was the first success and it boosted his belief and confidence. Again we refused donations and told him that he could pay us back by helping someone else down the road. About six months later, he was regaining some personal power and had the opportunity to help someone else. That was the second main success. From then on, he improved fairly quickly and understood that healing is a continuing process for all of us.

There must be an equal exchange of energy between healer and the person in need. This is part of the team effort and reflects the natural flow of energy through the multiverse. Whether that exchange takes the form of money or something else, it must be sufficient to maintain balance and continue the cycle of healthy energy through the relationship.

This can often be part of the learning experience for the healer. Many of us who deeply feel the service aspect of the shamanic vocation feel as though we should simply give it all away, receiving nothing in return but the knowledge that we have been of service. That is a nice sentiment but it can easily turn into a martyr complex. It is also not realistic and does not empower the individual in need of healing.

Those who seek out shamanic healers need to recognize their own responsibility in the process as part of the team. They cannot simply suck up all the good energy and move on. That disempowers the relationship and dishonors the process. When someone accepts his or her own responsibility and consciously chooses to maintain balance in any relationship, that individual necessarily becomes more powerful.

Integrity and honor create personal power. We develop our own integrity when we are honest in any relationship; when we act like adults and take responsibility for our actions and our needs. People of integrity do not feel the world owes them anything. They recognize their role in the creation of their experience of reality. This is the relationship we want to foster through our healing service. This makes the process easier and more effective for all concerned.

How you choose to structure your healing practice is entirely up to you. I merely recommend that it be a conscious and self-aware decision. If your choice feels pressured or somehow uncomfortable, you are not ready and need to go back for more personal work. Being of service does not make one a servant nor does it put one in power. Both partners must be truly honored through the process.

Healing for Friends

I should say something here about working with friends and acquaintances. When a friendship becomes a healing partnership, the dynamics are likely to change. The possibilities inherent in this change must be examined and discussed in depth before you choose to add that new element to your relationship.

A friendship that becomes a healing partnership can strengthen a relationship. Your friendship can provide additional trust and belief that will aid the healing process. To make the jump to Healer can also destroy a relationship that is already tenuous or strained. This change in dynamics has the potential to create tension in any relationship. Once you don your Healer hat, you are no longer simply the Friend. The status quo of that relationship cannot remain the same. This may raise or exaggerate issues related to control or self-esteem. Those who tend to perceive themselves as perpetual victims may feel that you as Friend are deserting them and you as Healer don't understand their needs. They can resent you for not getting drawn into emotional dramas.

Furthermore, as a shamanic healer, you are constantly communicating with spirit guidance. The normal controls of a friendship may impede the effectiveness of the healing process. There may be things that you simply do not say to some people in your life. You may have developed a particular role that would conflict with the role of Healer. Once you agree to be of service as a shamanic healer, you must honor the guidance and message you receive from the spirits.

Many healers have lost friends or acquaintances at various stages of the healing process. The reasons are widely varied and may simply be the result of growth and change that causes one or both individuals to move on and away from the relationship. However, friends or acquaintances may expect you to make things easy for them.

There are always people who resist any advice or perceived criticism you may offer, but friends may expect you to fix things for them without any pain or real growth on their part. They may just want a soul retrieval or an amulet that will make their life better. Sometimes they want your help in convincing those around them to change while they remain the same. Frequently, they want the healing to occur in one session. They may get upset when a lifetime of problems does not disappear over the period of a week or a month. This is particularly true with families in crisis.

These are very individual situations that must be handled with as much integrity and honesty as possible. Preparation for working as a healer with friends and acquaintances might include a very open and honest discussion with the individual requesting assistance. Make it clear that while you are willing to help, your role must change if you are to be effective. If communications have been less than completely open and direct, let this person know that things may change. The bottom line is that these individuals asked for your help. You do them a disservice and dishonor your spirit guides if you allow the "rules" of the relationship to dictate the shamanic working.

On the other hand, you must honor your feelings and reactions. If a friendship ends as a result of the process, you should genuinely strive to be there if and when that person is ready to reopen communication. If an honest feeling of openness and caring is not present, the reasons for that must be investigated before re-establishing the relationship.

A Team Effort

It is important to recognize that healing is a team effort. The team includes both shaman and the individual in need of healing. It is commonly understood that this individual's belief and involvement is vital to the success of the process. People have been known to effect spontaneous healing on their own with strong enough beliefs. Someone who implicitly trusts a healer is more likely to be receptive to the healing work. On the other hand, an individual is quite capable of blocking all healing energy.

The healing team also includes the helping spirits of those involved. All of these beings work together to create a change in the energy of the person in need, whether this person is consciously aware of them or not. Calling upon this person's spirit guides as well as your own guides is an important preparation for any healing.

It is for this reason that I prefer to begin with a short discussion on shamanic perspectives and general energy anatomy when working with people who have little or no exposure to metaphysical concepts. This can create a basis of understanding that opens up communications. In short, it allows us all to speak the same language.

While you are acting as Healer, you must keep in mind that the family and community of the person in need also play a role in healing. They can support the process, coming together and lending energy to its success. They can be there to listen or simply sit with a family member who is in the process of healing. They can be strong and encourage a loved one to continue with the work, or to avoid detrimental situations when necessary.

The family can also make it difficult or even impossible for the healer to create any lasting benefit. This is particularly true for children and teenagers. A family that is hostile and refuses to participate in the healing process can effectively undermine the progress of a person living in the same home. Even a family that appears to be supportive of the work you are doing with a loved one can affect the energy in the house if they resist their own growth and healing.

I worked with one particular family that illustrates this situation quite well. I was friendly with Bob, the father, and knew the mother casually. They had a ten-year-old son who was experiencing terrible nightmares and was withdrawing more and more into himself each day. They also had a sixteen-year-old son who was getting into all kinds of trouble, including arrests and expulsion from school.

Bob was experiencing anxiety attacks and had begun to withdraw into alcohol more and more. The mother was in denial about her addiction to prescription Valium and she frequently retreated from the family into a drugged state. Bob asked me to work with his sons. His wife was not really shaman-friendly, but went along with it since their family therapist decided that it couldn't hurt.

The boys and I began a very simple course of taking long walks and learning about energetic interconnections. We had begun some simple breathing techniques and made it a point to attune to the Spirits of Place wherever we stopped to rest. Things were proceeding fairly well when all hell broke loose.

The boys were having difficulty being open and honest because their father insisted on always being present. He was openly critical of them much of the time; more so when he had been drinking. The boys withdrew even more until conversations were nonexistent, yet the father refused to allow them to speak with me alone. He said he wanted to be sure we were all on the same page.

To make matters worse, I found out that the mother was becoming increasingly fearful of the pagan implications in our work. She alternated between open hostility and increased Valium use. This created such stress on everyone involved that the boys began to feel guilty and protective of their mother.

Finally, it became necessary for me to have a very direct discussion with Bob about all of this. As honestly as I could while still trying to be supportive and optimistic, I explained all of my concerns. I told him of the possibilities and of the potential consequences. I made it clear that if things remained the same, I would need to stop working directly with them. I would remain a friend and would be there if any of them needed me. He told me that I was cold and hurtful.

Bob felt that I was trying to get out of working with them. He told me that I had no business commenting on anything but the metaphysical work we were doing and felt that I was overreacting to his drinking, which he insisted was purely social. He said that since he was their father, he knew what he was doing and believed that I should follow his lead.

Unfortunately, we were not able to move through this situation at the time. However, our friendship survived this situation. Over a year later, Bob contacted me again. He said that he felt he was coming from a place of guilt and defensiveness at the time. He was actively participating in Alcoholics Anonymous and the family was still working with a family therapist. His wife was still not prepared to have me in their house again so the topic of working with this family was not broached. It is interesting to note that Bob asked me to pray and journey for them on my own, which of course I did.

When situations like this arise, we must release the need to succeed or to control the situation. We do not fail if the individual or the family ends the process. This is a partnership that may be dissolved by either party. Releasing our attachments is vital to our own process of growth. It is also necessary to release this situation to the multiverse for completion.

These situations are not common, but they can arise and you should be prepared for the possibility. Preparing oneself for the potential psychological or emotional reactions of the individual, family, or community is just as important as any form of training we may receive. This is one reason why many healers recommend including psychology or some counseling classes as part of a healer's training.

Preparing for Healing Emergencies

Clearly, preparation and training are vital to the healing vocation, but there are many times in which there is no time to prepare. We may be faced with an emergency situation that requires our immediate focus. Many healers find that their responses to this type of situation become automatic over time. Some even have premonitions that their services will be required sometime that day.

In these events, a healer must be able to find focus very quickly, releasing fears or beliefs about how to prepare. Many healers say that their only preparation in these situations is a deep, centering breath. I have developed a physical anchoring technique, based on exercises I learned in the Silva Method and through neuro-linguistic programming, which causes my energy field to automatically clear and ground in times of need. These anchors that so many methods make use of today have their origins in the mudras and magickal postures or hand positions that have existed for millennia.

What this means is that I have conditioned myself to go through an energetic clearing and grounding in response to a physical stimulus. Much like Pavlov's dogs, I have developed an automatic response, except that I try not to drool. I use a type of hand posture as a stimulus to signal my energy body.

Whenever I put my thumb together with my second (middle) finger, I enter an altered state, and without any conscious control, my energy runs through the EarthStar exercise. I don't have to think about it and can focus fully on the situation at hand. You will find that, in time, you automatically put those fingers together whenever you have the need.

The easiest way to create this physical anchor is simply to use it whenever you perform your preferred method of clearing and grounding. Through continued use, this anchor will become associated with that state of consciousness. This is true for all ritual elements. Over time, we become conditioned to their use in a certain setting and respond to that association as we would during ritual.

If you prefer a more direct method of creating a physical anchor for yourself, you may use the method outlined below. As preparation for this, you will need to decide what your anchor will be and the specific responses that it will trigger. Set up your ritual or healing space as you would for a deep, profound ritual. Have ready anything you may need so there will be no distractions or interruption of the energy. Have a glass of water present on your altar or somewhere easily accessible within your ritual space.

CREATING A PHYSICAL ANCHOR

Purify your ritual space in your preferred manner. Create sacred space using the method that is most appropriate for you.

Invoke your spirit guides, the Creator, and any other spirits or deities you feel are appropriate. Your intent is to create a deeply healing space as well as personal clarity and grounding.

Drum yourself into a light trance. If you do not use the drum, count yourself down from ten to one, twice. It may help for you to visualize yourself descending one step with each number.

Become aware of your breathing. Observe it for a few moments. If you still feel any areas of tension, direct the breath to these areas until they relax.

Now begin to increase the duration of your exhalation until you have attained a 1:2 ratio between inhalation and exhalation. If you find you are gasping for breath on the inhalation, reduce the length of the exhalation. This should flow naturally without creating stress. Stay with the breath until you feel your trance deepen.

Place your hands or body in the form you have decided will be your physical anchor. Take a deep breath and focus completely on this anchor. Feel the physical sensation— the skin against skin, the pressure—whatever it is that this posture feels like.

Allow your focus to expand to include your trance and the energy of the room. Feel this energy create the anchor and feel the anchor create this energy. They are bound; integrated parts of one complete experience. Breathe into this feeling.

If you want to create more specific associations with this anchor, such as the experience of a particular meditation, bring those elements into your ritual now, while holding the anchor position. Perform the meditation, call in the deity, do whatever it is that you want to occur automatically when this anchor is activated.

Once again, allow your focus to expand to include your trance and the energy of the room as you felt it during this last step. Feel this energy create the anchor and feel the anchor create this energy. They are bound; integrated parts of one complete experience. Breathe deeply into this feeling.

Tensing the anchor position, say to yourself and to those you have invoked that this position will automatically create these conditions in your energy field whenever you take this position. State with intent that you will automatically assume this position without conscious thought whenever you have need of these conditions. State that this physical posture anchors these conditions in your physical body. Repeat this twice.

Ask the assistance and guidance of those you have invoked in deepening this anchor. Thank them for their presence and blessings and release the sacred space in your preferred manner.

Note: Make it a point to use this anchor each time you create similar conditions, perform your chosen meditation, or invoke your chosen deity. Continue to do this until you feel it becoming automatic.

From reading this chapter, it should be clear that our preparation for healing is multidimensional and ongoing. It includes the short-term, daily rituals we perform before healing and our personal shamanic work. It also encompasses the lifelong process of learning and growth. The Healer should not be seen as the ultimate end, the culmination and epitome of perfection and clarity, but rather as someone who has answered a calling and is consciously following the path toward wholeness.

All of us can be healers in a way, as we explore our own shadows and create more integrity in our lives. Simply through living a more honest life, we contribute to the healing of everyone else on the planet at this time. Even if you do not choose a professional healing path, know that your every action affects the rest of us. When your actions are made in a sacred manner, you bless and heal us all.

3

THE HEALER'S TOOLKIT

The toolkit is comprised of all those methods and items we feel are necessary or potentially beneficial in our work. This chapter deals largely with the physical items that a healer uses. While these items will obviously vary with the healer and tradition, there are some items that are commonly used today.

There are some tools that we use that are so involved they require a book of their own. These cannot be adequately covered in a page or two in this chapter. For this reason, several tools or methods have their own chapters within this book. These include techniques commonly associated with energy work, the use of dreaming, the drum, and those techniques involving the shamanic journey itself, such as extraction and soul retrieval. For more information on these and other tools, see the Recommended Reading section in the back of this book.

Most beginning healers love to go shopping for their craft. Healers that have been practicing for some time still love to shop, but they are generally more practical about it. Of course, they already have a basic toolkit, so shopping is a bit different for them, but all healers take great joy and pride in selecting just the right objects for them. We all love to buy Cool Metaphysical Stuff. That is why so many bookstores often make more money on ritual and decorative items than on books. We bring our enthusiasm with us into the stores or to the festivals, along with our credit cards and checkbooks.

Some people still believe that only items that are crafted by the healer or are received as gifts should be used. If you believe this is true, then it is true for you. No matter what you believe, the right items will find you.

My dear friend John recently shared the story of how his fan came to him. This fan is the tool that he uses the most and is sacred to him. This sharing was the first time he related this story and I am honored that he would allow me to share it with you now.

It all started with two dreams during which his spirit animal led him on a path that had crow feathers on it. In the second dream, John gathered up the feathers and made a fan of them. Upon awakening, he made a sketch of the fan. He pondered this for a few days and forgot about it.

Several weeks later, this same spirit animal came to him and directed him to drive to the park on the outside of town. John was told there was something waiting for him there. After "several minutes of struggling with the logical mind," he got in the car and headed for the park, laughing at himself the whole way.

When John got to within one-quarter mile of the park entrance, he saw a crow lying dead on the side of the road. He had instinctively taken a plastic bag with him and brought the crow home in this bag. John realized that the crow had not been there for long because rigor mortis had not set in.

John sat with the crow for a long time, amazed at its beauty and the fact that it was there for him. He made a spirit connection and asked for permission to honor it through the creation of a fan from its wing. Permission was granted, provided he use both wings and give one fan away.

He said many prayers and removed the wings with great care. He wrapped the crow's body in a cloth and buried it along with several gifts and many prayers. About three years later, John found the owner of the second wing.

He met a friend of a friend who was a Wiccan high priestess. When John met her, he knew that she was to have the other fan. He had grown attached to it, but remembered his vow to the crow spirit. He gave it to her at a Samhain celebration and she was speechless. He was filled with joy in that act of giving away. He could "hear Crow cawing with delight."

It may or may not amaze you that someone would bring home road kill for a sacred purpose, but I know a surprising number of people who recognize the gift in this and choose to honor the spirit that has departed rather than simply drive by. This is more common than you might think and it is a beautiful method of releasing and honoring a spirit. This is far better than recognizing that once again we humans have caused a death and put it out of our minds without another thought. In this way, we strengthen our connections with All That Is and give a departing spirit a sacred gift.

Many people prefer to find their tools through stores or festivals. I knew a woman who had been searching for a drum for quite some time. She considered making one but had no idea where to begin and could find no classes in her area. Although she is not a big garage-sale shopper, she and her husband stopped at a garage sale one weekend. It was obvious that the homeowners were metaphysically inclined from the books and crystals for sale.

Out of the sun, in the back of the garage, the woman found a small frame drum. On its surface was a Celtic spiral in the colors she had been dreaming about for weeks. She had no doubt this was her drum and immediately purchased it. She feels this drum called to her somehow and pulled her to the garage sale. She works with it regularly and considers it to be one of her best friends. (See chapter 6 for more on the shamanic drum.)

The point is that once you put the thought out there and begin to look for your tools, they will find you. It may take some time for the right ones to manifest, but you can trust that they will do just that. Whether you find them in a garage sale, create them yourself, or receive them as a gift, it is the honor and intent with which you use them that counts.

The Healing Altar

Most shamanic healers have some form of altar in their homes or in the healing room. This is often our focal point when asking for guidance and assistance. It is also the place where we honor those allies that work with us and bless our actions. Some of us keep our most sacred healing and ritual items on the altar.

The altar is commonly home to tools for trance induction and the specific work at hand. Some of the things you will find on a shamanic healing altar include a Spirit Dagger or ritual knife, a Medicine Bowl, and a Ceremonial Cup or Chalice (see Figures 1, 2, and 3). The bowl and chalice are used to bring in the water element, for spellwork, for offering libations to the spirits, and for scrying. The bowl may also be used to make potions or incenses and to create a healing matrix (see page 83). The dagger is used, among other things, to create sacred space and remove intrusions.

An altar is a permanent sacred space. It is a very special creation of love and respect. It may become a daily reminder of your vocation and your spirit guides, or it may be a method of holding sacred space in your home. It can also function as a physical home, to some extent, for the energies of your helping spirits.

We have several altars around our home. Each has a different focus. I have always kept my Medicine pouch and healing stones on my main altar. However, when I made the decision to complete this book after having worked on it sporadically for two years, I had an experience that caused me to create a very special healing altar.

At the time I was working with a women's full moon circle. We were from varying spiritual backgrounds and occasionally offered rituals based on our individual traditions. There were four druids in our group, three of whom combined our druidry with other paths. On

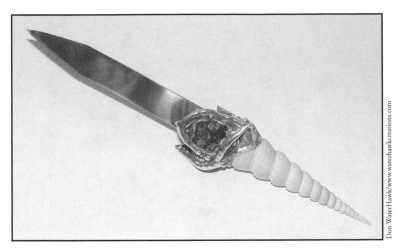

Don WaterHawk/www.waterhawkcreations.com

Figure 1
Spirit Dagger for cutting cords, creating sacred space, and removing intrusions.

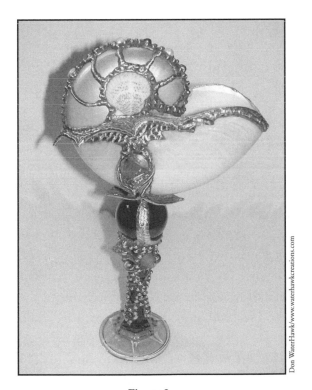

Don WaterHawk/www.waterhawkcreations.com

Figure 2
Ceremonial Chalice for making offerings and charging spells.

Don WaterHawk/www.waterhawkcreations.com

Figure 3
Medicine Bowl for scrying, making potions, and sending healing energy.

New Year's Day 2000, we druids got together to prepare an Imbolc rite dedicated to Brighid.

I never felt a particular connection with this goddess and was feeling some resistance to dedicating myself to Her. I had too much work to do already as a field biologist and no time to concentrate on yet another goddess. The ones I currently worked with were enough for me for now, I thought. Apparently, Brighid had other ideas about this.

Throughout the day, the hostess druid smelled something odd. She couldn't quite place it, but knew that it was not normal for her home. At one point, it became so intense she decided we had to find the source. I looked over to see my leather jacket on top of her humidifier. It was one of those plastic ones that emits steam to humidify a room.

The steam and heat from the element had ruined the front of my jacket. The leather had constricted and there was a huge dark stain. Brighid, as goddess of fire and water, had chosen to mark my cow skin jacket. In Celtic myth, the cow is sacred to Brighid. This was simply too much to ignore, particularly in light of my earlier resistance to this dedication.

I went home and meditated on this situation. It was clear that this was a message, sent to someone that was thinking way too logically and not listening to Spirit. I took the pocket from the front of my jacket where the leather had stained and become almost pleated, and created a pouch dedicated to Her. Although I did have to miss our ritual, I received one of the candles lit by a member of our group who is a Sister in the *Ord Brighideach*.[1]

Since that time, I have transferred this flame to a special candle that sits at the center of my healing altar. Also on this altar is my Brighid pouch along with several stones and other items that are integral to my path as a healer. This is a very special altar, dedicated to all my helping spirits, but the central space is held by that goddess who chose me—and did so in a way that could not be ignored.

A Healer's Bookshelf

Shamanic healers tend to be avid readers. Most of us start early on collecting those books that we feel are valuable resources for our growing reference libraries. The library of a healer is likely to be comprised of a wide variety of books.

Most healers will have books on herbs, stones and crystals, homeopathy, bodywork, and energy work. They are likely to have books on anatomy and physiology, psychology, and nutrition. Certainly, there will be good books on shamanism and probably a variety of other traditions as well. Field guides are a must for anyone who plans to collect native plants.

In a healer's library you may find books that do not appear to be related to healing at all, such as books on biology, environmental science, philosophy, and even physics. People who work with a variety of ethnic groups may have foreign language dictionaries or books on those specific cultures. There is likely to be a book or two

---

1. A Brighidine order of flame-keepers.

on divination, possibly accompanied by a tarot deck. To a healer, particularly a shamanic healer, health and healing involve far more than antibiotics or specific techniques. We heal the total person and every aspect of life is applicable.

The healer's bookshelf will also contain the healer's own journals. I highly recommend the use of a specific healing journal. This is a special place for you to record healing dreams or journeys that either still need interpretation or have provided some valuable information, possibly in the form of symbols. The journal can function as a type of symbolism dictionary.

The healer's journal can also be used to record the healings you are led to perform and their effects (see Figures 4 and 5). In time, this will develop into your own "medical" reference book. Years later, when you encounter a similar case, extensive journeying or divination may not be necessary. Your guides may lead you back to your own book for the cure. This is a wonderful way to train your children or anyone you may be guided to mentor.

Herbs

All shamanic healers use herbs to some extent. Some healers may only use them as teas for colds or other simple ailments, while others may use them extensively, both internally and externally. Herbs are also used in spells and for purification.

Many of our modern medicines are derived from the chemicals found in plants. Some people believe that herbs are as harmless as homeopathics. It is true that using the whole herb, rather than its derived or synthesized chemical component, is generally more harmonious to the human system, but it is also true that herbs are medicines and can have powerful effects.

It is very important to research the herbs you intend to use, particularly if you are prescribing for children, pregnant women, or nursing mothers. Herbs are one case where more is not necessarily better.

Case Details

Date _____   Time _____

Name _____

Contact Information _____

Main Complaints _____

_____

_____

_____

Discussion Points _____

_____

_____

Spirit Guidance/Intuition Received During Discussion _____

_____

_____

_____

Healing Action Taken _____

_____

_____

_____

Spirit Guidance/Intuition Received During Healing _____

_____

_____

_____

Follow-ups Planned _____

_____

_____

_____

Homework_____

_____

Figure 4
Shamanic healer's journal—case details.

Trance Work

Date _____   Time _____

Case/Name _____

Shamanic Journey/Meditation/Dream (circle one)

Intent or Focus (if applicable) _____

_____

_____

Details _____

_____

_____

_____

_____

_____

_____

_____

Messages Received _____

_____

_____

Relevance to Case _____

_____

_____

Unknown Symbols/Images _____

_____

_____

Intuited/Possible Meanings _____

_____

_____

Next Step(s)_____

Figure 5
Shamanic healer's journal—trance work.

They tend to work gently. As a result, you may not see an immediate effect. It is a good idea to start with small doses when working with children or particularly vulnerable individuals. Watch for signs that the symptoms are improving before increasing the dosage or switching to another herb.

Rescue Remedy is one of my favorite treatments, both for children and adults. We have used the cream for burns, cuts, rashes, insect bites, and injections. The tincture is good for just about anything that may cause fear, trauma, or stress. I even use this externally as a treatment for stress when working with wild animals.

Externally, we use herbs for smudge, incense, and offerings to the spirits that guide and help us. These are readily available in health food stores and many metaphysical shops. Many of us prefer to use local herbs because they resonate with the energy of our home area. Some of us will harvest local plants. Many healers also tend wonderful herb gardens.

WILD PLANT WALKS

There is one strong caution I would give anyone planning to embark upon a medicinal or edible plant walk: do not put anything in your mouth until you are absolutely certain what it is. It is vital to educate yourself on the poisonous plants in your area and learn how to identify them. A good rule of thumb is: if in doubt, don't touch it.

Unless you are an expert at mushroom identification, never taste or eat a wild mushroom. Mushrooms contain a multitude of complex chemical compounds. Many of these are harmless, some are hallucinogenic, and many are dangerously toxic.

If you are picking plants that you plan to ingest in any form, it is also advisable to avoid areas that are close to highways. The plants near roadways will absorb both the airborne exhaust of passing vehicles and any petroleum products that leak onto the ground.

Many species of edible or medicinal plant life bear strong similarities to poisonous species. Ingestion of many of these other species can be debilitating, even fatal. Unless you are highly skilled at identification, I would recommend avoiding any of the similar species in the wild.

Begin by choosing a place that you may be confident has not recently been picked. Take along a paper bag for collection, your field guide, and any offerings you may want to leave in return for these herbs. Offerings may include a gift of water, other sacred herbs, corn, or simply a blessing and sending of loving energy. Be mindful of your choice of offerings. We want to honor the spirits of the plants and the Earth Mother, not litter.

A paper bag is preferable to a plastic bag for drying plants, although it doesn't really matter what you collect them in. Plastic bags retain the moisture of plants, preventing drying and increasing the possibility of mold growth. You may also wish to hang plants to dry.

Once you get to the area you are going to harvest, take some time to be quiet and center yourself. Ask permission from the Spirits of Place and wait for an answer. If you get an uneasy or doubtful feeling, try another spot or go home. Find the oldest bush in the area and leave your offering there. This may be a bush that is obviously larger and older, but it may be just a feeling that you have. Then take a small piece of sacred herbs (if edible) and put it in your mouth. As you chew on this, go wherever you are led for harvesting.

Be sure to pick only as much as you need, and not to take too much from one bush. Move on until you either feel a clear signal that you have taken enough, or until you have the amount you set out to collect. Leave an offering at each bush you harvest from, along with a prayer of thanks.

When you are finished, return to the oldest bush and give thanks for the gifts of these herbs. Promise to use them in a sacred manner and to always honor the spirits of the land. Then return home and keep your promises.

Animals

Many shamanic healers make use of animal parts in their work. These may take the form of leather pouches, a necklace of claws or teeth, or specific parts to be used for specific methods. Earlier in this chapter, I discussed the fact that many of us will utilize the bodies of those killed along roads or found in the wilderness. Very few modern shamanic healers kill for their parts. Some do hunt for food and take only what they need in a sacred manner. Afterward, everything is used and nothing is wasted.

Alternatively, I know a few people who use photos, statues, and museum-quality replicas of animal parts to bring in the same energies. I have used these myself on occasion and find them to be highly effective when these energies are called into the object and when my belief is high.

Certain animals are known for their healing energies. Bear, frog, and beaver are among those animals honored as healers among native cultures. A bear's tooth pressed against a pain was frequently used to heal the cause of the pain. I was once drawn to use wolf fur in an amulet for a man suffering from lupus. Whether because of the amulet or his belief in these methods, afterward he gained some real relief from his symptoms. Even modern medicine uses parts of animals, such as shark cartilage, in healing.

These body parts are viewed as sacred gifts to be honored. They bring us the energies of the species from which they came, much like various healing stones bring in their own different forms of energy. Like many other tools, these are sometimes purchased by the healer.

I would only make two recommendations regarding the use of animal parts. First, educate yourself on the regulations of your state or country. Many species of animals are legally protected and it is illegal to possess these body parts. This includes feathers from most wild birds. Certainly, many people have small collections of feathers they found lying on the sidewalk or in the woods, but it is your responsibility to know the laws and the potential consequences if you are found with illegal body parts.

Second, be very careful when purchasing animal parts. The sacred uses we have for these items do not justify abuse of the living animal. Ignorance of where the animal part came from is no excuse. As shamanic healers, we are responsible for respecting and caring for all living beings. We must be careful that we do not create a demand for body parts that come from abused or endangered animals.

Because of the legal issues involved, I will not go into great detail about the use of these parts. There are several books available on the energies associated with various animal species. These books can be good guides in developing your own methods of use.

Feathers and feather fans are commonly used in smudging and beautiful fans are sold at most pagan and metaphysical bookstores. I have a few friends who also use feather fans in moving energy and opening chakras. Many of us have been taught that certain types of feathers are powerful tools for cutting attachments and cords, including cords binding us to past-life events. The feet and talons of some birds are also used in pulling cords from the energy field, while the cord is cut with a ritual knife, such as the Spirit Dagger (see page 49).

Many people will use feathers, fur, or skin as a ritual cloak or for ritual masks. In this way, we may bring in the energy of specific animal allies as well as honor those that guide us. The teeth and claws of certain mammals are also used in various healing spells to impart strength or draw out an illness. Various animal parts will also hold places of honor on our altars out of respect for our personal animal allies.

Homeopathy

I highly recommend homeopathic healing. I have used it since I was a child and it continues to work wonders for my entire family. Homeopathy is an involved discipline requiring years of study to practice it well. However, it is true that you cannot overdose on homeopathics. I would caution you that some negative effects are possible. The only possible drawback is that the wrong remedy has the potential to create the symptoms it is intended to treat in an individual who does not already exhibit those symptoms. The truth is that this is a rare occurrence, and usually the worst that will happen is nothing.

This can be such a powerful healing method for both emotional and physical complaints that I would recommend getting a few books on the subject or taking a class in homeopathic healing. Most remedies sold in stores are combinations for specific conditions or complaints that are listed on the side of the bottle. The combination may not be exactly what you need, although it is likely to give some relief. It is also true that the individual remedies work on far more symptoms than the few listed on the label. A good book can be a great help in narrowing down the perfect remedy.

Bodywork

Bodywork is a general word that can mean anything from massage and shiatsu to acupuncture and cranial-sacral therapy. The various forms of bodywork can release repressed issues, keep energy flowing through the body, and maintain the health and vitality of all physical systems.

In chapter 9, I describe a method for releasing soul fragments in the physical body. Bodywork can serve the same function, either on purpose or spontaneously. Many people, including both my mother and I, have even experienced spontaneous past-life memories that were evoked by a bodywork session.

When soul fragments have been stored in the body for a very long time, perhaps for lifetimes, or when these fragments contain a significant emotional charge, they may resist release without assistance. This is equally true of energetic intrusions, which are foreign energies that have taken up residence within our energy fields. Exercises designed to allow us to recover soul fragments on our own may not always work. Bodywork can be a highly effective alternative to the soul retrieval or extraction journeys.

I am aware that this may be an uncomfortable technique to use, particularly with older children and anyone who is not comfortable with physical contact. This is one reason it is extremely important to treat those that come to you for healing as partners and discuss your recommendations in advance. If you feel that bodywork is called for, yet the person refuses it, you must honor his or her wishes and seek another way.

Diet

A chapter on diet could easily become at least one entire book on its own. Therefore, I will not write in great detail regarding specific conditions that can be controlled through a change in diet. Suffice it to say that these conditions can be anything from diabetes and hypoglycemia to cancer and attention-deficit disorder.

Many of these conditions often mimic behavioral problems or biochemical imbalances. As a result, a healer might consider having specific tests done if an individual shows signs of ADD, extreme depression or moodiness, postpartum depression, body tremors, and even psychosis. Speak with a physician or research the symptoms yourself. Use the shamanic journey to determine the correct tests and dietary changes. Special nutritional or blood analyses may indicate a nutritional cause.

A well-rounded diet that is low in refined sugars, processed foods, preservatives, and pesticides is beneficial for each of us for many reasons. Not only does it contribute to a healthy body that is more capable of fighting off disease, but it also allows us to maintain greater control over our emotions and our energies.

Exercise

Most people in modern society are not vigorously active on a regular basis. This lack of physical activity begins in childhood and increases dramatically during adolescence. Our children learn from our example and most adults feel that they don't have enough time to work out after answering the demands of work and family.

While many adults are trying to lose weight, most do not enjoy physical *exercise*. They perceive exercise as being time-consuming, boring, and physically painful. On the other hand, physical *activity* is often viewed as fun and enjoyable.

As healers, we need to be aware of the benefits of physical activity, both for those we are called to heal and ourselves. Regular moderate activity can substantially reduce the risk of developing or dying from heart disease, diabetes, colon cancer, and high blood pressure. Moderate levels of exercise appear to reduce the symptoms of depression and anxiety, improve one's mood, and enhance one's ability to perform daily tasks throughout life.

Regular moderate activity is the key. We can play, hike, or work around the house, as long we do it consistently. Certainly, the benefits increase with the duration, intensity, and frequency of exercise, but the average person can improve his or her health, future, and attitude just by having some fun away from the television set.

Healers may experience an additional benefit from moderate exercise. Exercise and play help us to release tensions and stresses that may interfere in our workings as shamans and healers. Many of us find that we are more capable of meditating and working effectively in ritual after some form of exercise, partially due to an increase in specific biochemicals called endorphins. Exercise, laughter, and orgasm are some of the best ways to consciously make the body produce endorphins.

Endorphins are biochemical painkillers with a chemical structure like morphine. When they are released, they bind to the opiate receptors in neurons, blocking our experience of pain and increasing our experience of pleasure. They affect the flow of other biochemicals, which play a part in allowing the body to experience altered states.

Endorphins are largely responsible for "runner's high" and that great feeling we get from orgasms. Some of the sacred plants used by shamans and other ecstatics across the world also release endorphins. Many people feel as though they are automatically lifted into altered states once their production of endorphins is increased, most notably after exercise.

As healers, it is in our best interest to take part in some form of physical activity on a regular basis. It is also beneficial to recommend moderate, but consistent physical exercise to those that come to us for healing. Following through on this, as well as on other exercises we might suggest, is part of each individual's responsibility as a partner in his or her own healing.

Breathing

The benefits of breath control, also known as *pranayama,* are innumerable. I cannot recommend the benefits of developing an awareness and control of the breath highly enough. If you are a parent or work with children, this is one of the greatest tools you can teach them. This is also extremely important when working with anyone in pain or nearing death.

This is an area in which I believe any shamanic practitioner, particularly a healer, really should become proficient. If I were to rate training for shamanic healers, this would be in the top three requirements. As Alan Hymes, M.D., writes, "The effects of breathing extend to the workings of the heart and lungs as well as to subtle physiological interactions such as the molecular processes through which the body's energy production is maintained."[2]

2. Rama, Hymes, & Ballentine, *The Science of Breath,* 25–26.

The impact of the body on the breath, and the breath on the body, becomes obvious during an emotional outburst. When someone is frightened or very upset, he or she begins to breathe more quickly and from the chest. Unfortunately, chest breathing is quite common during normal functioning in Western society. The shallowness of chest breathing reduces oxygen intake and fatigues the body-mind. This effectively puts the body and mind in a state of constant anxiety and stress.

On the other hand, the breathing of someone who is calm and centered is significantly different. During these times, the breath fills us from the diaphragm through to our shoulders. We breathe slowly and deeply. It is no surprise that when we want someone to calm down, we inevitably tell them to "take a deep breath" and relax.

As Swami Rama describes, the "science of pranayama is thus intimately connected with the autonomic nervous system and brings its functioning under conscious control through the functioning of the lungs."[3] This is the one exception to that rule we were all taught in high-school biology, that the autonomic nervous system processes are involuntary. This is also where a healer may derive the greatest benefits.

Through the conscious control of inhalation and exhalation, and through maintaining diaphragmatic breathing during everyday life, we can regulate our responses to trauma, pain, and more. By the simple control of the breath, we can remain calm and centered. In teaching these methods to those we are healing, we provide them with a significant tool to handling their own pain and fear.

Below I outline three exercises that are ideal for anyone learning to control the breath. Each of these exercises is very simple and will encourage the experience of calm and balance. These are particularly recommended for anyone who is experiencing pain, fear, difficulty saying good-bye, or difficulty letting go of this lifetime. I also recommend

---

3. Ibid., 95.

these techniques to anyone involved in the death process of a loved one, before or after death.

BREATHING EXERCISE 1

Place your full attention on your breathing. Do not attempt to alter it, just observe it for a few moments.

Where does your breathing seem to come from? How do you feel at this moment? If there is any tension in your body, where is it localized?

Now slow your breathing. Count to three on each inhalation and again on each exhalation. Breathe deeply, filling your lungs from the bottom first. Feel your diaphragm stretch and expand as your abdomen moves out. As you exhale, feel your abdomen contract as the breath leaves from the bottom of your lungs first.

Breathe into any areas of tension or stress. Feel your breath fill and relax these areas. With each breath, tension and pain melt away.

Once you feel comfortable with this exercise, increase the count for inhalations and exhalations. Practice this several times a day, particularly when you are feeling stressed or are in pain.

BREATHING EXERCISE 2

Beginning with Breathing Exercise 1, begin to alter the count of inhalations and exhalations. Starting slowly, work toward a 1:2 ratio between inhalations and exhalations. For example, if your inhalation lasts for four counts, your exhalation will last for eight counts.

Do not increase this ratio too quickly. If you are gasping for air and desperately sucking in the inhalation, you should return to Breathing Exercise 1.

BHRAMARI

Breathe in deeply through your nose. Breathe out also through your nose, but exaggerate a nasal buzzing or humming sound, like that of a bee.

Repeat for a maximum of three minutes. If necessary, alternate with Breathing Exercise 1.

Spells

Some people don't think of spells as being shamanic in nature. They are popularly perceived to be more a part of witchcraft or sorcery. Since shamanism was traditionally a total lifestyle that encompassed a great many other aspects of the life of a medicine man or woman, it is not so surprising to find that many shamanic, indigenous cultures used a variety of spell techniques for healing.

The use of speech in various forms is the most common method of shamanic spellwork. Incantations are used to entice illness or spirits to leave, bind energies to a person or object, invoke deities and helping spirits, induce trance, and evoke the ability to heal the Self. Because of the multitude of uses for the voice of the shaman, I have chosen to devote chapter 7 specifically to this. Incantations are covered in that chapter.

One form of spell that is commonly used among shamanic peoples is the magickal transference of an illness or pain from the body of the person in need into an external object which is then buried, burned, or otherwise cleared and discarded. For example, a cure might involve the placement of a burnt piece of wood over an injury or area of pain. Some cultures actually place a piece of wood or a ring over the area and burn it on the body. Through this process, the illness is transferred to the wood, which is then burned in a ritual fire to release the sickness.

Illnesses were believed to have a variety of sources. Spirits or curses may bring sickness. Violation of social taboos and the loss of personal integrity were often seen as the cause for certain illnesses and injuries. Many cultures saw illness as originating in the elements or from natural sources. Even extreme emotions, if left unhandled, were believed to cause sickness or attract injury.

Like homeopathic healing, the cure for many of these illnesses lies in the cause. If the illness was believed to have been derived from a certain area of land, a small piece of that earth would be removed and pressed against the wound or area of pain while an incantation was spoken. The earth was then removed and returned to its home. The Earth Mother cleared the illness and the person in need and the land were healed. This was a common practice with diseases of the skin among native peoples.

The making of dolls or representations of an illness or injury is another common form of healing spellwork. Usually one, three, or nine dolls are created for a healing. As the doll is created, the essence of the illness is bound to the doll. Sometimes the doll is rubbed on or placed over the area of concern. Other times an incantation is used to bind the illness to the doll. In some cultures, a wooden doll is infused with this essence. As the wood rots or burns, the illness is released from the person in need. The dolls are also discarded at crossroads or in water to disable the disease or send it far away.

Some spells are direct commands for an illness to leave the body, while others take the form of trickery or even short stories. The candle spells used by many pagans today can be quite effective when used for healing. For a spell to be successful for healing, both the healer and the person in need must believe in it. Since few people in modern societies have any real, deep belief in the power of spells to cure, this method has lost popularity. I would invite you to experiment with spellwork for yourself and see how it works. You may decide this is an effective method you can include in your healing toolkit.

Divination

Most shamanic healers use the shamanic journey as their primary form of divination. They enter the journey in search of clues to causes of illness and guidance in how to proceed in healing. The journey is also used to consult the spirit of the person we are called to heal as well as the patient's spirit guides. We don't always have time for a full journey, however, and sometimes we want a simpler method of gaining insight into a healing.

Card Decks

Most modern healers work with some type of divination card deck. Some have more than one deck. While I almost exclusively use one deck these days, I will occasionally use other decks for specific types of questions or for additional perspectives. Other times, I just use whatever deck I am drawn to for a particular case.

For the shamanic practitioner, a divination deck can offer greater insight than is possible simply through a spread and a reading. However, this benefit can be achieved with any deck, particularly one you feel connected to and have worked with regularly.

If you are experienced at shamanic journeying, all you need to do is take an important card from your spread and enter the journey with the card and its placement within the spread in mind. Use it in place of, or to complement, a specific question in your journey. Allow this image to take you where it will.

If you are less used to the journey or prefer a more guided visualization, use your creativity and understanding of your cards to outline a meditation based on the image. For example, say you drew the Tower in the Future Outcome position in a tarot spread. Your visualization might entail coming to the Tower at the end of a trip through the current situation and ascending the Tower to find spirit guides, answers, or a new path beyond this experience. Make it as detailed as you want or allow it to be a bit more open for a true shamanic journey to develop within it. If you choose a detailed meditation, you might prefer to tape-record it to follow along with in trance.

The Pendulum

Some people will use the pendulum for divination, which can include divination for diagnosis. The pendulum can be used quite effectively for identifying blocked or imbalanced chakras. It is not absolutely necessary to use the pendulums that are sold in stores. These can be quite expensive and may be no more effective than a ring hung on a chain.

When using a pendulum to diagnose areas in need of attention, it is simply held over the body at a height of two to three inches. The pendulum is slowly moved along the body, stopping at any chakra point, joints, organs, or anywhere you may believe there to be an energy imbalance. Open to your intuition and watch for any unusual motions by the pendulum as you move along.

It is best to clearly identify the symbolism of the various movements a pendulum may make. This will vary with the person and the pendulum, so it is a good idea to make this clear each time you use one. A good beginning is to ask what motion will indicate a "yes" and a "no." For healing work, you may want to identify the motions for imbalance, block, injury, and so on.

It is important to keep it simple. A pendulum can only make so many different movements so you may want to do a general yes/no reading first, followed by a more specific one. This way a circular, clockwise motion may mean one thing in the first reading and something else in the second reading.

These same methods can be applied to divination without the presence of the person in need of healing. You can use your basic yes/no response for a series of questions related to the case at hand. The use of one or more pendulum charts is very effective in clarifying issues or areas to explore, particularly when the individual in need is not present.

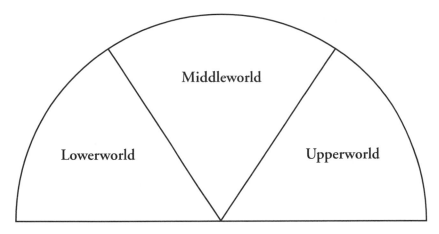

Figure 6
Three Worlds chart.

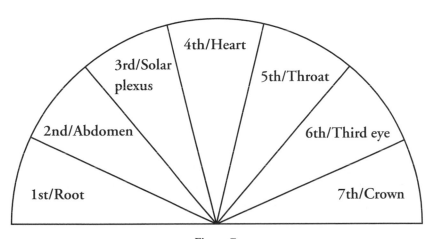

Figure 7
Seven chakras chart.

This method consists of holding the pendulum above a chart and meditating on the case or question. The pendulum will begin to move and will be drawn over one or two areas more frequently or more intensely than others. These are areas that should be explored more in depth.

See Figures 6 and 7 for examples of these charts. They can be modified to suit your particular needs. They may include charts to determine what chart to use or what methods to use in proceeding: astrology, bodywork, and so on. The charts you need will quite likely develop spontaneously through your own practice.

Augury

Some of the more traditional divination methods involve the use of rocks, clouds, or the actions of wildlife, particularly that of birds. All of these methods spring from our innate connections to All of Life. We attune ourselves to the natural world and find guidance and answers in the symbols we see.

The world itself is not usually rearranging itself to offer us answers. It serves as a canvas for the projection of our inner knowing and spiritual guidance. The images or animals we observe may or may not be new, but it is our awareness and interpretation that is expanded, allowing us to work out these situations a bit more objectively on an external focus.

Divination through observing the behaviors of wild animals can take a great deal of experience and knowledge of the animals you have chosen to observe. Although an animal will suddenly appear and the message will be clear, this is not a common occurrence. I will not deal with this method in this book because of all that it involves. It is not something that can be taught through a book. If you are interested in this method, I recommend learning as much as possible on the species in question from both scientific and metaphysical sources. Then begin your observations as a spiritual field biologist. Record normal behavior along with anything unusual. Make detailed notes as well as drawings, and photographs if you can. Document your own feelings and any messages you may receive in relation to your location or the actions of the animals. Over time, you will come to know their ways and you will develop a shamanic connection to them. You will know unusual behavior or appearances and possible reasons for them. You will also be able to call upon their wisdom for guidance through your connections.

When divining by rocks, clouds, or other natural objects, we employ a form of scrying. Scrying is a method of seeking answers through focusing on a bowl of water, a glass of brandy, a polished black surface, or a flame. We sit in silence for a moment, grounding and centering. Then we focus on the question and ask for guidance. We open our eyes and focus this question on the scrying surface. We begin to see images—perhaps symbols, faces, or even events—in the object. These images are then applied to the question, if the answer is not already apparent, and meditated on further if necessary.

Drum Divination

There is one divination method that makes use of the drum and was derived from the practices of some circumpolar peoples, most notably the Saami. This does not appear to be a common practice. In fact, I know of only a handful of people who have experimented with this method.

The first step is to determine the "map" you will create on the surface of the drum, as well as an indicator that works best for you. For a map, you might choose to separate the drumhead into the three shamanic worlds and include other symbols that might be beneficial, such as spirit guides, times of day, and so on. You might choose to include a World Tree or chakra system in the center of the drum for additional guidance. I know people who use different drums for Upperworld and Lowerworld journeys, or specifically for healing work. These drums would be expected to have differing symbolism or maps. These are merely suggestions. You might try experimenting with different maps covering your drum before creating a permanent one on the head itself.

The indicator works like a pendulum, although it moves to the drumbeat rather than completely on its own. The drumhead functions as a type of guiding chart. Indicators may take any form, provided they do not interfere in any way with the functioning of the drum or your focus during the session. This would eliminate anything that is so flashy it will distract you or so large that it is not clear what one symbol it has landed on. You should avoid anything that might mar or damage the head of your drum.

Once you are ready to begin, simply place your indicator in the center of your drum and begin to beat slowly and monotonously. Be careful that you do not allow your drumming to influence the indicator. Again, you will want to experiment with the best way to beat and hold the drum for you. It may also take some practice to be able to enter the trance and encourage guidance to come through while maintaining an awareness of the progression of the indicator.

I have created a timeline along the outside rim of my drum. I either beat the drum at the place for the time of year the session takes place, or I will start the indicator at that place rather than in the center and beat around it. Most of the time it does not matter which method I use. Both tend to have very similar results. However, for certain people or situations, one method does feel more correct than the other.

Interpretation will also be a personal issue. If you are highly in tune with your drum, you may intuitively understand the reading without having to memorize the symbols and the order in which they came through. Even if this is true for you, it is likely that some of the time you will need to interpret.

Often the meanings will be rather obvious. A reading for a friend on the verge of divorce may go the Realm of the Dead or symbols indicating pain or fear. This will show you the death of the relationship and of the relationship self, along with the associated emotions. Where the indicator proceeds next will give clues as to what will come after or what issues need to be addressed for healing to occur.

Sometimes the symbols may mean nothing to you, but the person in need of healing may have immediate reactions to them that hold the key to growth and understanding. This is true of any divination system, particularly the card decks. Perhaps your question had to do with a job difficulty and the indicator passed through the Snake symbol. You may interpret this as energy, life force, sexuality, and so on, while the person you are reading for immediately says, "Yeah! That's my boss, the rotten snake!"

This is merely an overview of some of the more common methods used by shamanic healers. It is far beyond the scope of this book to delve any deeper into the majority of these methods, although I have devoted full chapters to a few of them. I offer these as suggestions for your exploration. You will find, over time, that your toolkit will develop into a highly personal one, containing some of these and probably several methods not even mentioned here.

The most useful tool a healer has is open communication with spirit guides. When this channel is clear and open, you will have access to all the answers you need. Your guides may guide you directly, or they may lead you to other people who are teaching methods you need to learn. In any event, they are our greatest asset and should be honored and respected for their part in our growth and development.

4

ENERGY WORK

Healers and medicine people from all over the globe have used a variety of techniques to heal with the personal energy field. The existence of electromagnetic fields produced by living things and the earth is commonly accepted today. Within the human body, biochemical processes produce electrical impulses that are measured using a variety of cardiac and neurological diagnostic machines, including EKG, EMG, and EEG. Techniques such as acupuncture, Reiki, and shiatsu have been developed to work specifically with this energetic field.

In modern society, we generally think of the Eastern cultures, particularly those from India, when we discuss this type of energy. We think of the chakras and their associated energy bodies that became a part of Western consciousness with the introduction of Eastern philosophies. The truth is that many cultures understood the chakra system and used it for healing. While the words may change and the images may vary, this is an aspect of healing that is part of our collective history.

The use of healing stones has been documented in almost every ancient society. Crystals in particular have been honored and utilized by medicine people and shamans throughout the world. Many cultures have been known to work with manipulation of the physical body, whether through massage or some form of reflexology.

All of these methods have a significant impact on the personal energy field. In modern times, other methods have developed with the same goals, including Reiki and toning. The method you choose is not as important as your dedication and level of success. Trusting instinct is wonderful, but the majority of these methods do require training and study to be truly effective.

The human energy field is vital to our existence. It permeates the physical body and interconnects us with the universal energy field— that which binds us to All of Life and all worlds. Many of us have heard the phrase "Thought precedes action." This is a simplistic way of saying that everything that occurs in the physical realm is caused by events occurring in the purely energetic realms of existence.

What occurs within our energy bodies has a direct effect on the physical and vice versa. Although physical events may have their precedent in the higher energetic realms, an energetic memory of these events is often stored in the physical body, along with any uncleared trauma and fragmented soul parts. The spirit carries these residual elements beyond death and often into the next incarnation. Working consciously with this energy is an excellent way to clear old patterns and memories that may be causing current conditions.

Healing Stones

Special stones and crystals have been used by healers throughout the centuries. Some shamanic cultures believed that the shaman held a special crystal within his or her body. Several Native American peoples used crystals extensively for healing and divination. Sacred stones have been used in just about every culture on Earth.

Most people who work with stones find that the stones hold energy and information. Furthermore, they amplify energy and may impart specific attributes to the wearer. Many of us wear jewelry with specific stones that feel right to us or carry the vibrations we wish to bring into our lives. Some of us will carry a stone or two in our pockets. In the home of a healer, stones can be found just about everywhere.

Using Crystals

Quartz is the second most abundant mineral in the Earth's crust and it can be found in nearly all acid igneous, metamorphic, and sedimentary rocks. Many of the healing stones that are commonly used are forms of quartz. Quartz crystals also possess piezoelectric properties, meaning that they develop positive and negative charges on alternate prism edges when subjected to pressure or tension. This means that quartz crystals can convert mechanical vibrations, such as sound, into electrical signals. This can be particularly effective when coupled with drumming, song, other music, or incantation.

As a result of the piezoelectric effect, quartz crystals have been used in many different types of electronic communications, including radios and television, clocks and watches, and even in cigarette lighters and ammunition detonators. For healing purposes, piezoelectricity is one of the means by which crystals transform energy. In the hands of a healer, this transforming energy may be directed to specific complaints or the crystal itself may be used to transmute illness into health.

Many healers find that a crystal will grab unhealthy energy like a hook. In this way, crystals are often used to remove intrusions, blocks, or other energetic imbalances from the auric field of a person or animal. The crystal is not always capable of lifting all the unhealthy energy at one time. Therefore, it must be cleared between applications.

I have used this method on both humans and animals and the process is always the same. For example, every year I receive several birds that have been attacked by cats. Cat attacks are surprisingly dangerous. If the initial physical injuries do not kill the bird or puncture one of the air sacs causing it to suffocate, the bacteria on the cat's claws will set in and create a potentially deadly infection.

I have had good success using crystals for the infections caused by cat attacks on birds. I have used it on everything from finches to baby owls. When an infection has set in, I prepare the room for a healing ceremony. I treat the bird with Rescue Remedy for stress and do whatever is necessary to keep the bird calm. I enter trance and look for the energetic imbalance or intrusion. When I find it, I use the crystal to hook or scoop out this unwanted energy.

I remove as much as possible with one slow swipe or swirl of the crystal. When you do this, you will probably feel some resistance or tingling in the crystal. If you do not *see,* you will need to practice *feeling* it. Once I have it, I submerge the crystal in blessed water (see chapter 6) or salt water. This releases and holds the unhealthy energy. I then have a second bowl of specially prepared water to purify the crystal in before returning it to the animal's body. For humans, I often have smudge burning and use this as my second purifier, but most animals find the smoke stressful. I repeat the process as many times as necessary to completely clear the unwanted energy. Since the sound of a drum would be potentially stressful to an animal, I follow up by using my hands or a new, purified crystal to direct healing energy into the area previously occupied by the unwanted energy.

Crystal Attunement

There are a variety of ways to attune to a new stone. Attunement can be important to the healer before using a stone in healing work. If you are accustomed to silent meditation, you can simply sit with the stone and open to any impressions or messages that flow from it into you. If you tend to remember your dreams, keep the stone with you as you sleep. Use the dreaming techniques in this book and maintain a dream journal during this time. Before falling asleep, focus on your stone and ask it to speak with you that night.

Unless you have been trained in specific methods, the best way to begin working with stones is to keep one or two on or near your body as much as possible, and to meditate with them. If you are working with a specific stone, you will need to keep it with you at all times for at least twenty-four hours; some people say seven to thirty days. This imbues the stone with your personal energy. It also permits an attunement to develop, synchronizing your energies with those of the stone, and allowing healing to begin.

If you choose to prescribe certain stones as a treatment for the people you work with, you will need to give them a short course in crystal attunement and clearing. You may choose a stone for them or send them off to a store to find a specific type of stone on their own. As long as they know how to properly clear a stone, it doesn't matter which route you choose for them to obtain their stones.

Many shamanic healers prefer to use the shamanic journey or lucid dreaming to connect with the spirit of the stone. We hold the stone as we enter the journey with the intent to communicate with the spirit of the stone. Once we meet with this spirit in the journey, we ask if it needs further clearing, how we might honor it best, and how it might be used most effectively. We also ask if it has any guidance or messages for us. When developing a relationship with a new healing stone, we keep up this dialogue through journeying and dreaming until we feel so connected that conscious methods of contact are no longer required.

If you prefer a more guided visualization, this one has always worked well for my family.

CRYSTAL ATTUNEMENT EXERCISE

Begin by inspecting the stone. Feel it and look carefully at it from all angles.

Count down from ten to one or enter a light trance in your usual way.

See the stone before you, at least as big as a house. Walk around the outside of it and inspect the object from this perspective.

As you walk, you find a door in the side of this stone. Ask permission to enter. If permission is denied, return to normal consciousness and try again at a later date.

If permission is granted, enter through the door, giving thanks as you enter. Take note of the light and temperature inside the stone. Be aware of everything you see and feel. Do any beings greet you? Explore the inside of the stone, taking note of everything as you go.

When you have explored everything or are ready to return, go back to the door through which you entered this stone. Take one last look around. Leave an offering of some sort and say thank you before exiting through the same door you entered.

Count back up from one to ten or return to normal consciousness in your usual way.

There are some basic concepts to keep in mind when working with any type of stone. The termination, or the point, indicates the direction of energy flow through a stone. This is true for any faceted stone. The angles and shape of the facets give direction to the energy. Some people believe that facets also increase the magnitude of the energy. Crystal or other stone balls send out a smoother energy flow in all directions. Crystal clusters tend to radiate group energy. They can bring harmonious energy into a room or a home.

Many of the stones used in healing are also associated with the various chakras, generally based on color. These stones can be extremely beneficial when placed on the chakra or used during a meditation specific to that chakra. See Table 1 for a basic chart of chakras, colors, and commonly associated stones. Table 2 describes the general associations for each individual chakra.

No matter how we work with the stones, it is important to honor and respect them. Many people see them as the Stone People. We ask permission before using them and give thanks afterward. Even if this

TABLE 1

Colors and Stones Associated with the Seven Major Physical Chakras

Chakra	Color(s)	Associated Stones
1—Root	Red or black	Garnet, black tourmaline
2—Abdomen	Orange	Carnelian, amber
3—Solar plexus	Yellow	Citrine, tiger-eye
4—Heart	Green or pink	Jade, rose quartz
5—Throat	Blue	Turquoise, blue topaz
6—Third eye	Indigo	Lapis lazuli, sodalite
7—Crown	Violet	Amethyst, purple fluorite

TABLE 2

General Associations of the Seven Major Physical Chakras

Chakra	Associations
1—Root	Spinal column, kidneys Survival, physical sensation, passion
2—Abdomen	Reproductive and lymphatic systems Sexuality, ambition
3—Solar plexus	Stomach, liver, adrenals Will, manifestation, intuition, intellect
4—Heart	Circulatory system, thymus Emotions, love, healing, nurturing
5—Throat	Lungs, throat, thyroid gland Communication, creativity
6—Third eye	Ears, eyes, nose, pineal gland, lower brain Inspiration, psychic sensitivity
7—Crown	Pituitary gland, upper brain Out-of-body travel, direct Otherworldly experience

is not your belief system, they should be treated with honor, as you would any ritual tool.

Clearing Stones

Even stones that you have had for a while should be cleared periodically. Some stones, like amber, must be cleared more frequently due to their tendency to absorb negativity. Other stones, like diamond, are notoriously difficult to clear. To make it easier, I recommend frequent clearings.

When I was younger, the most popular way to clear stones was to bury them in salt or soak them in salt water. This is still beneficial for clearing stones. However, I have read studies that indicate certain crystals lose some of their piezoelectric properties when exposed to salt. Salt can also mar the surface of some of the softer stones, although generally this does not affect their abilities.

My favorite ways to clear and purify stones and crystals are smudging with sacred herbs, burying them in earth for seven days, and using running water over them. The smudge ceremony is outlined in chapter 6. Burying them and running water over them allows the elements to purify your stones naturally. You might use the water from your sink or spend some time submerging them in a stream. When using any of these purification methods, visualize all unwanted energies breaking up and leaving the stone as you carry out the action of clearing. Continue until you feel the stones are clear and ready to work with you.

My good friend West Hardin created the wonderful tool below, the Crystal Healing Matrix. It is based on a method he found several Reiki practitioners using for distant healings. He altered the process and offered it to our journeying group for experimentation. Everyone loved it and I am honored that he is willing to allow me to share it in this book.

The Crystal Healing Matrix is based on the premise that the mineral world will hold, receive, amplify, and project energy. Through this matrix, we can program our healing intent to support us in our own work or we can use it to send healing to a specific person. The sand and stones also hold the energy. This eliminates the need for constant re-energizing. It seems to almost function as a battery and alternator system. The energy that is received from the healer is held and recycled as it is also directed to the person in need.

If at all possible, ask for permission before sending healing energy to another person. The reality is that this is not always possible, but never attempt to force your own needs or beliefs on the people you are called to heal. Always keep in mind that the energy you send will be used according to the individual's choice and best interest. We cannot heal another without their participation or permission on some level of being.

CRYSTAL HEALING MATRIX

You will need:

- A broad, shallow bowl
- Sand
- Stones and/or crystals
- A large "generator" crystal
- Smudge
- A smudge fan or feather

Smudge yourself, your work area, and the objects you have collected for the creation of this tool.

Fill the bowl about halfway with sand.

Draw a spiral into the sand.

Holding your hands over the sand, ask it to awaken and share its blessings.

Smudge the bowl once more.

Place the stones in a circle around the rim.

Smudge each stone once again, touching each with your smudge fan or feather. Ask each stone to awaken and share its blessings.

Awaken the generator crystal as you have the others and ask for its blessings.

Place the generator crystal in the center of the bowl.

You may also add other crystals and gemstones to the bowl as you wish, perhaps at the directions to draw in the healing energies of the quarters.

Charge the bowl as a unit with your energy and intent. Ask these stones to work together for the benefit of your healing work. Trust that the matrix will continue to generate your energy and intent.

For Distance Healing:

Holding a small, single-terminated crystal, visualize the person, plant, place, or animal to which you wish to direct healing. See and feel a connection develop between this crystal and the object or being of healing intent. Ask that this healing be for the highest good of all involved.

Set up the matrix as above. Place the crystal in the sand facing whatever direction you feel is most appropriate.

Draw a line in the sand from the center crystal out to this crystal and connect them by charging the bowl with energy once again. Trust that this healing energy will be continually directed to the person in need.

Although the matrix does tend to produce its own energy, it is best to check on it each day and recharge as you feel necessary. Sometimes it will need to be recharged every day, sometimes not for several days. It is also important to maintain an awareness of the status of individual crystals. Depending on the healing at hand, crystals may need to be occasionally removed from the matrix for clearing. Individual crystals should be removed when the healing intent has manifested.

Healers tend to develop collections of stones that work best for them as individuals. Many stones are commonly used, but it should be noted that not every healer uses them for the same reasons. There are healers who find that the common associations found in books or websites for particular stones do not fit with their experience. I may find that amethyst catalyzes change in all aspects of my life, while my colleague may find that this stone brings healing, but not necessarily any other type of change.

For this reason, it is best to use the references as guides. Experiment and discover what works best for you. Creating your own healer's reference based on your experience will produce the most valuable book you own. When I was fifteen, I created this type of reference for stones, metals, and crystals for my parents and myself. Although it has been revised and added to over the years, we still use that book today.

In Table 3, I offer some associations for commonly used healing stones. These associations are drawn from my experience and that of the many healers I know. Your experience may vary. The associations

---
TABLE 3
Common Healing Stones

Amber	Purification and protection, patience, aids in recovering past-life memories and soul fragments. Needs to be cleared frequently.
Amethyst	Catalyst for change, elevates energy to a higher level, connection to spirit guidance and personal intuition; magnifies energy of wearer.
Aquamarine	Protection, meditation, calming influence.
Azurite	Connection to spirit guidance, creativity, relaxation, aids in dissolving energy blockages.
Bloodstone	Courage, strength, trust, aids in situations of change.
Carnelian	Stability, harmony, increase energy and physical vitality. This stone has been known to catalyze or increase an ability to channel spirits and should be used with caution by those possessing these tendencies.
Chrysocolla	Heart healing, emotional healing, reconnection with Nature, encourages self-esteem and self-love.

(continued)

(Table 3 continued)

Citrine	Protection, transforms negative energy, energetic balance, stability, manifestation, clarification. Rarely needs clearing.
Clear quartz	General healing, magnifies energy, connection to spirit guidance and personal intuition.
Fluorite	Stability, balancing, purification, particularly effective in physical healing. Color variations have additional associations.
Hematite	Grounding, protection, concentration, mental clarity, transforms negative energy, balancing, cooling and calming.
Jade	Dreaming, harmony, access to spirit guidance, emotional strength.
Jasper	Protection, energy balancing and stabilizing. Different forms have additional associations.
Lapis lazuli	Intuition, psychic awareness, connection to spirit guidance, creativity, dreaming, protection.
Malachite	Transforming, emotional clarity and healing, balancing, protection, general healing.
Moonstone	Reflective, introspective, intuition, empathy, cleansing, connection to one's feminine side, calming, nurturing, sustaining.
Obsidian	Grounding, reconnection with Nature, protection, aids with focus and journeying, especially Lowerworld journeys. Variations hold additional associations. Needs to be cleared often.
Pearl	While not a true stone, pearls are wonderful for strengthening a connection to one's feminine side and one's emotions; also clarity, integrity, depth.
Rhodochrosite	Energizing, purification, balancing, stimulating.
Rose quartz	Heart healing, unconditional love, gentleness, calming.
Smoky quartz	Grounding, special ability to ground the spiritual into the physical, dissolves negativity, protection, stabilizing.
Sodalite	Mental clarity, decision-making, connection to spirit guidance.

(continued)

(*Table 3 continued*)

Tiger-eye	Mental clarity; access to memory, grounding, balancing.
Topaz	Confidence, creativity, connection to ancestors and spirit guidance. Colored variations have additional associations.
Tourmaline	Clearing, energizing, transforming, balancing, protection, self-confidence. Colored tourmaline plates only allow certain rays of light to pass through, absorbing most ordinary light rays. Crossing two of these plates will block all light. This is a wonderful stone to use for selective protection, circle energy, and specific healing. Colored variations have additional associations. The dichroic stones offer the balance of the color combinations.
Turquoise	Protection, inspiration, strengthening, grounding, aids in communication, connection to spirit guidance or master healer, especially a spiritual connection.

found in reference books may vary as well, but they are likely to be more inclusive than I have room for in this book.

Color Healing

Disturbances in the personal energy field may appear as discolored or disfigured auras. You may see a dark area or a color that is not quite clear or true. Sometimes thought forms are visible within the energy field of a person. More traditional shamans may perceive these as embedded spirits, insects, or animals.

The easiest way to heal with color is to simply channel clear, white energy to the individual in need. If you see disturbances in specific chakras, you may wish to channel the pure color that is associated with the healthy chakra. If the disturbances appear to be an excess of energy in that area, you may prefer to channel the opposite color for a balance. The use of the drum for energetic imbalance is discussed in more detail in chapter 6. Refer to Tables 1 and 2 earlier in the chapter for associations with the seven chakras.

Many people instinctively use color energies through the selection of stones and clothing or home decorations. For example, when I am on my Moon (menstruating), I tend to prefer pinks that make me feel comforted and loved, blacks to balance out the red in my root chakra and to ground me, and deep earthy green for grounding and comfort. Many women wear rose quartz at this time of the month for the same reasons I wear pink clothing.

As a healer, you can use this to your advantage in decorating your healing space and deciding on your dress for healing sessions. You can also recommend that the people you work with incorporate a color into their home or wardrobe for a period of time that will help balance them. This may also be a factor in the types of stones you suggest for healing.

5

DREAM WORK

For many people, native and otherwise, dreaming holds the key to power and health. Dreams often tell us far more about an illness than any physical symptom. As a result, traditional shamans tend to be extremely interested in the dreams of those they are called to work with—not only current dreams, but all dreams going back months or even years before illness manifested.

Dreams not only give us clues to cause and cure, but they may serve as warnings. Premonitions of injury, illness, and death often come to us through dreams. For example, my mother and I were warned through our dreams of the type of illness that would cause the eventual death of my grandfather years before he fell ill. His circulatory problems appeared to us as rivers and streams. Later on, near the time when he would be admitted into the hospital, the rivers in our dreams turned polluted, giving us clues to the sepsis infection that eventually killed him.

There have been times when I was far too tired from mundane reality to engage in a fully awake journey. At these times, I used dreaming to gain insight into a case or situation and to obtain the knowledge or guidance I needed to determine how best to proceed. I have trained myself to awaken with full recall after the dream I intend. I write down the dream in as much detail as possible and return to much-needed sleep.

According to Victor Sanchez, the Yaqui shaman don Juan Matus said that dreaming is the "best avenue to power because it is the door that leads directly to the nagual, returning us to the unknown and mysterious side of our awareness."[1] For don Juan, dreaming is "a bridge to the other self, helping to unite the two sides of awareness . . ."[2]

No matter what your feeling may be regarding Carlos Castaneda's research and writings, the teachings set forth are valid and several other people have come forward as students of the man known sometimes as don Juan. It is true that many have questioned Castaneda's methods and even the reality of what he reported. I was once told that one need not accept the teacher to benefit from the teaching. This is a good mindset to take in this case if you question it since many people have truly benefited from these teachings.

For many people, dreaming is the closest they come to shamanizing. During dreaming, the rational, analytical mind is shut down. This allows that "bridge to the other self" to open. It permits us to retain memories of out-of-body travel and communication with spirit guides. In ancient times, it was believed that only shamans could direct their dreams. This is no longer the case. Modern people are learning to use their dreams and to consciously direct them.

Lucid Dreaming

Lucid is generally defined as "easily understood, clear," even "rational" and "sane." When applied to dreaming, it means that we take the rational mind into dreaming with us. We are able to control the direction of dreams while we allow them to spring from the source of

---

1. Sanchez, *The Teachings of Don Carlos,* 177.
2. Ibid.

our inspiration. Simply put, lucid dreaming is active shamanic journeying while the physical body sleeps.

Members of my family tend to use dreaming a great deal. Most of us receive warnings in dreams, such as those received by my mother and I regarding my grandfather. Many times potentially dangerous situations were avoided by listening to the lucid dreams of family members. Each of my Elders has shared powerful dreams of prophecy, teaching, and exploration. They have taught me to trust lucid dreams and have spent many hours cautioning me against analyzing them away. To my detriment, I did not always heed these teachings.

Lucid dreaming is a powerful tool for the healer because it unites the two sides of awareness. We have access to our rational minds, but the truly analytic side of us is shut down during dreaming. We can think but we do not automatically reject things we do not want to see or that appear to be too weird to believe. Inspiration and direct communication to spirit guides permeates dreaming. Yet during lucid dreaming, we also have the ability to direct the dream and focus on a particular healing case or condition.

Modern people sometimes find that lucid dreaming is best done from a specific starting point, much like many people will begin the shamanic journey from a certain hole in the ground or tree. This provides a known image that we can actively move toward. In this place, we feel safe and in our element. From there, it may be easier to journey forth in search of the answers we need. We may also find that within this special place, we have all the access we need.

Below is a method for creating an astral clinic. This may be thought of as a healing office in the Otherworld. It may simply be the place you meet your guides and start out from, or it may become all that your office and healing room in this world is—with additional access to knowledge and energies. Like lucid dreaming, this method is part active creation and part opening to inspiration.

This astral clinic is based on a combination of techniques my parents and I learned in the mid-1970s. We refined it over the years to best fit our style of working. This is such a valuable exercise that we all still use our astral clinics today, more than twenty-five years later. In your healing practice, this can be taught to anyone, even children, to assist them in establishing relationships with spirit guides.

CREATING THE ASTRAL CLINIC

Hold in your mind the intent to create a special healing space for you and your guides in the Otherworld. You may want to create this at your favorite place of relaxation or near the World Tree. Count yourself down from ten to one or enter trance in your usual method.

When you reach your chosen place or have attained a suitable trance state, ask for the assistance of your guides. Then imagine a room or building that will be ideal for you to heal and gain the information or wisdom you need to heal yourself and others. Use active imagination in creating the perfect place for you. You may see it first from the inside or outside. If you first see it from the outside, enter into it as soon as you have completed the outside.

Create the inside exactly as you want it. You can always change it as needed, but create something to begin with now. You might have a special healing room or rooms, an office with a wall of file cabinets and a computer, a comfortable desk and chair. Imagine whatever you want into existence. Be sure to have a comfortable space for your guides and a special door or elevator off to one side. This will be your means of bringing in the people in need of healing, special healing guides, or other beings that may assist you in your work.

With your current guides in attendance, ask if there is any other being that would like to regularly assist you in the work you do. Allow some time for this being to enter through your special door or elevator. If no one shows up at this time, that is perfectly acceptable. If you feel that the being that has shown up is detrimental or dangerous, have him or her leave.

Thank your guides for their assistance in this creation, take one last look around, and return to normal consciousness using the same method you entered trance.

Even if no one showed up as a special healing ally, you might want to ask at the beginning of each healing session if there are any beings that can assist with the specific work at hand. You may find that occasionally the spirit of the person in need, an ancestor, a deity, or some other guide will arrive for that particular working.

Each time you use this place, your connection to it grows stronger and the benefits you derive from it increase. After a time, you may find you no longer need it. However, even experienced healers often use a special focal point such as this to increase the effectiveness of their work.

You may also be guided to assist those you are healing in creating a similar space for their own personal use. Modern meditation and hypnosis techniques generally refer to this as the ideal place of relaxation. This may be a healing garden, an office (provided there is no stress involved), or an astral spa of sorts. With guidance and practice in these methods, the person in need of healing can significantly contribute to his or her healing process.

The person in need of healing should be instructed to work with dreaming according to the outlines in this chapter. However, this person should be encouraged to keep a journal and discuss all dreams that occur during the healing phase with the healer. The interpretation may be obvious. There may also be subtleties present in the dreams that require the experience and direct connection to spirit guidance that is possessed by the healer.

With or without the astral clinic, we can utilize dreaming to obtain guidance and information. We can use it to establish a deeper connection with those in need of healing and with our own guides. We can also teach these methods to anyone we are called to heal so that they may facilitate their own healing and find long-term support for health maintenance. The exercise below is outlined for long-distance healing, but it can be altered to fit any purpose you need. It is to be performed immediately before falling asleep.

DREAMING EXERCISE

When you are in that sleepy frame of mind just before falling asleep—where you feel just on the verge of sleep but are still aware of this world—visualize the person in need of healing standing before you. Be aware of the environment in which you find this person and any other beings in attendance.

Take a good look at the energy field of this individual and note his or her actions and words. Ask the individual and/or his or her spirit guides for any information that will assist you in helping this person regain health. Ask for permission to direct healing energy to the person in need this night.

With focus and intent, tell yourself you will remember this dream when you awaken. Then allow yourself to drift off to sleep.

It is a good idea to keep a pad of paper and pen next to your bed. People often awaken immediately after the dream meeting and will usually lose the memory if they fall back to sleep without recording it.

Initially, some people may have difficulty with dreaming exercises. Many of us do not remember our dreams and, if we do, we generally believe they are nothing more than the psyche replaying or working out events from this reality. We don't remember how to bring them back into our waking lives so we don't. As a result, dreams are often automatically filtered out of waking consciousness.

We all have the ability to eliminate this filter. The blocks to dreaming are learned; we were not born with them. These are the same blocks that prevent most people in modern society from consciously using the shamanic journey. The dreaming body is the free soul. It is this energy body that we take with us when we journey out of body.

Therefore, dreaming is shamanic journeying. They are one and the same. The only difference is that during dreaming the physical body is in its daily period of hibernation, allowing the free soul to wander at will without the need for trance induction.

If your initial attempts at lucid dreaming do not appear to be very productive, I strongly recommend sticking with it. In addition to your dreaming exercises, work with the breathing exercises. Additional practice with the shamanic journey while you are awake is another excellent tool for learning control over dreaming. Each of these techniques is guaranteed to significantly benefit your personal toolkit.

The keeping of a dream journal is also very beneficial. In this initial journal, you may prefer to record any sensations or experiences that are associated with your dream exercises. Many people associate feelings of motion or vibration with lucid dreaming and astral travel. When you notice a pattern beginning to emerge through your exercises, use that to develop dreaming techniques specific to you. Keep in mind that we are relearning a skill that was lost many years ago. With practice, it will return.

Dream Interpretation

The need to interpret dreams has sparked a plethora of books, websites, and classes. Many of these are quite good, and some are far too rigid to be of value. The truth is that while much of the symbolism we receive during dreams and journeys may be interpreted according to common or cultural beliefs and myths, often it is our personal symbolism that comes through.

A perfect example was recently presented by two friends of mine. One friend was involved in a business deal with an unsavory character who made regular practice of lying in both her personal and private lives. Over several dreams and journeys, Snake repeatedly visited my friend. He looked through all the animal symbolism literature and considered the possibilities. Our gut instinct, however, told us both that while we may see Snake as a potent and respectable being, there is another side to Snake energy that corresponds to the societal image of "snakes" as untrustworthy, mean people. It soon became clear after several journeys that his guides were telling him to stay away because this woman was that type of "snake" and could not be trusted.

Another friend of mine also experienced a Snake encounter. During a journey, she was trying to get a handle on her lover who kept changing his attitudes regarding some of the things she was doing. One minute he was supportive and interested, and the next he was shouting that it was all horrible and she needed to stop. In a cave, she watched a snake shed its skin over and over. The others in the group pulled out the books and tried to explain it based on this information. My friend considered this, but knew without question that the shedding of skin was his changeable nature and that this was not likely to stop in the near future.

To alter an old adage, sometimes a snake is just a snake. More correctly, those images and beings that are prominent in your dreams or catch your eye for some reason should be explored in your own subconscious as well as in the literature. A dream journal can be invaluable in clarifying your personal symbolism. Over time you will notice patterns of meaning, possibly in association with other elements of the dream.

In *Pagan Parenting*, I outline an exercise for parents to use to help children interpret their own dreams.[3] Not only does this hone our own accuracy and provide personal insight, but it also empowers each of us

---

3. Madden, *Pagan Parenting*, 38.

and allows us the opportunity to be our own psychics or shamans without having to rely on another person or a book.

In this exercise, the dreamer is encouraged to record everything that happened. As adults, we can obviously write it all down on our own or we may choose to use a tape recorder to document it. The goal is to get into as much detail as possible. Have a trusted friend or family member ask questions to spur your memory of additional details.

Make an attempt to recall as many aspects of the dream as possible. Try to be very specific about how you felt, what you were wearing, what colors you saw, and any associated smells, sounds, colors, and so on. Include those beings or objects that you experienced, the time of day or night, the location, any activity that occurred. Notice that I write "experienced" rather than "saw" or "heard." Sometimes in dreams and journeys other senses are awakened, allowing us to experience or know of a presence without seeing or hearing it.

Once the details have been recalled, begin to take the dream apart piece by piece. For example, if you saw a dragonfly land on a neon yellow car, use free association or the association web exercise (see chapter 8, Shadow Association Web Exercise) to evoke meanings you associate with dragonfly, neon yellow, and the type of car, or cars in general. Then interpret the scene as a whole. Taking the dream in this way— gradually interpreting from the pieces up to the whole dream—has proven very effective. Practice using this method with everyday dreams only increases your ability to interpret your own symbolism.

Nightmares

From time to time, even healers have to deal with the images and illnesses they handle each day. Sometimes this can build to the point that we experience nightmares. Certainly in an ideal world the healer will clear these issues as they come. In reality we don't always do that. The healer will generally have all the tools in this book and more to use in dealing with his or her own nightmares.

However, when we are called upon to help someone who is plagued by nightmares—especially a child—the handling of these situations can be a little tricky. While our first desire is to eliminate the fear and stop the nightmares, the dreams are clues to hidden issues. Even nightmares can be used as a way to join the two sides of consciousness and help us gain a deeper knowledge of Self.

It is normal for children between the ages of two and five to have some nightmares. These are generally believed to be the consciousness working through everyday changes in their life and mental/physical abilities. It is not so normal for adults and older children to have frequent or recurring nightmares. Even in younger children, recurrent nightmares should be investigated. Nightmares can be caused by tension, trauma, any type of change, the use of or withdrawal from certain medications, illness and fever, or by the bubbling up of repressed shadow aspects. Nightmares can also occur when we have attracted disruptive energies or get involved in astral difficulties.

When a nightmare is the result of a trauma, such as witnessing a disaster or violent crime, the dream state is often the best way for the consciousness to work through the trauma. Unless the dreams prevent normal sleep, create additional trauma, or continue for more than three months, elimination is rarely the preferred choice. We can supplement the healing action of the dream state, but we don't generally want to stop the healing work of dreaming.

The first course of action is to disarm the fear that nightmares may create. Some people with recurrent or frequent nightmares will be afraid to go to sleep. When they do sleep, they often retain that tension, which prevents a healthy and restful sleep state. Many of the techniques in this book can be used to reduce the stress created by nightmares. For example, working with masks, painting and drawing, and keeping a journal are all effective methods of externalizing the nightmare so it can be more easily faced and handled.

Protection methods can be extremely valuable in eliminating perceived or real threats. Purifying the energy of your home or bedroom, erecting a circle of sacred space, and calling in the protection of your personal spirit guardians and any home or place guardians are all powerful first lines of defense. This is particularly true when the dreams appear to be some form of psychic attack. These rituals also have the power to ease the mind and enable the individual to get to sleep more easily.

Nightmares can be acted out or turned into stories that similarly externalize and defuse the fear, particularly after several recitations. It may help to see your nightmares as stories, similar to those described in chapter 8. The ending of dreams can be altered in this way first. This often carries over eventually into the dream state, allowing even those who have not developed their abilities for lucid dreaming to alter the ending of a nightmare.

Even children as young as three can be coached to change the frightening aspects of a dream while they sleep. The more the story is rehearsed, the more it integrates with your consciousness, allowing you to remember it during dreaming. The technique used above to create the astral clinic can also be used to create special dream tools, such as magick wands, escape pods, or entrances for spirit guardians to enter the dream.

The key to completely eliminating nightmares is to decode the symbolism and handle the underlying issues that lie at the root of the dreams. The use of a dream journal and artwork such as painting, drawing, and sculpture, can be invaluable in learning the language of dream symbolism. As you work with these methods, some symbols will be immediately obvious while others will become clear as a pattern emerges. Frequently work with the dream interpretation techniques described above to develop your interpretive abilities.

It is clear that all dreams, including nightmares, can be valuable avenues to self-knowledge and healing. Through decoding this symbolism, we increase our abilities to interpret shamanic journeys and other visions or messages received during healing work. This benefits the healer and the person in need of assistance. This is such a powerful tool, all healers should be encouraged not only to add this to their personal toolkits but also to teach these techniques to those they are called to heal. This can only add to the power of the healing partnership.

The truth is that dreams occur whether we consciously ask for them or not. To avoid working with them and to avoid developing our lucid dreaming abilities is to refuse one of the most powerful tools available to us. As shamanic healers, we utilize all avenues open to us in order to effect the greatest healing for ourselves and those that ask for our assistance. Dreaming is possibly one of the simplest yet most powerful tools we have at our disposal. All we need to do is develop the ability and use it.

6

THROUGH THE DRUM

The drum pounds my heartbeat
Da dum da dum
I resonate with its energy as the tempo changes
Da da dum da da dum
It calls to me
Leading me away on my journey
A living cord of light and sound
Connecting me to this world
It stays with me, unseen
Then it cries for me
Dum da da dum dum
I am pulled back
Da da dum da da da da
Easily I return
On a path of light and sound[1]

Drums have a mystical quality to them that seems to touch us, even today. There is something about the rhythm of the drum that gets into our blood and makes us want to move. Thoughts of ancient

---

1. © 1990 by Kristin Madden.

and magickal cultures often evoke images of half-naked or ritually dressed people dancing to drums around bonfires. The effect a drum has on us is deep and automatic.

For many cultures, the drum has been the primary tool of the shaman for hundreds, even thousands, of years. Frequently, it was the drum that was used to induce the shamanic trance, allowing the shaman to leave his or her body and travel to other worlds or to move about unseen within this world. The drum has been used for divination and to invoke the spirits. It has been used to guide the departed spirits into the next world and to call them back for rebirth.

Silencing the Drums

Because of its close association with shamanism and its deep-seated emotional effects, fear of the drum has been a major focus of conversion tactics and ethnic "cleansing." In the early Christian church, all music was forbidden except for unaccompanied singing of the psalms. The pope outlawed the tambourine, a type of drum with small attached cymbals, in the sixth century.

When Africans were brought to North America as slaves, the slave traders understood the power of the drum for these native peoples. Not only were they used for spiritual purposes, but also for communication. As a result, African slaves were forbidden to make or use drums.

The shamanic drum of the Saami people was outlawed in the Scandinavian countries as a tool of the devil. It became a "terrifying symbol of the indigenous religion" for the clergymen that were attempting to convert the Saami.[2] According to Håkan Rydving, those people that were found to use the Saami drum in the 1600s were called to district court and were informed about the penalties for such use.[3] Henric Forbes wrote a scathing description of the drum

---

2. Rydving, *The End of Drum-Time,* 82.
3. Ibid., 56–57.

in the early 1700s. He wrote, "Oh you confounded Drum, tool and instrument of Satan . . . Each beat that is made on you, is and will be a Satan's beat in hell for them . . ."[4]

In spite of all this fear, majority cultures could not bring themselves to completely eliminate native drums. It is commonly known that drums were sold to museums and private collectors around the world. It is also said that Saami youths were occasionally sent along with the drums to "perform." Although these drums were feared, it would seem that our need for them continued in a rational, "justifiable" way through museums and other collections.

The Drum as Partner

Through the drum we can induce trance, let our spirits fly, connect with the Earth Mother, and heal ourselves and our communities. In the shamanic experience, the drum is a doorway. We may travel through it to other realities. Also and particularly when specific symbols are ritually placed on the drum, it may act as a gateway for invoking these energies or spirits.

The bata drums of Africa and Cuba are treated as living beings. There are very specific requirements regarding their care, feeding, and use. Furthermore, they are constructed in a ritual manner and the uninitiated are not permitted to touch them. The initiated must undergo deep training and progress up certain levels to play the different drums.

For many of us today, the drum is more than a wonderful tool. It is a living entity. For others it is a vital extension of the shaman and is respected as such. A drum may be perceived as a type of spirit guide, deserving of the same honor as our more animate guides are. Many people name their drums. This is not a silly affectation. It is an honoring of the spirit of the drum. These individuals will receive a name

---

4. Ibid., 81.

through journeying or meditation that they know belongs to the drum. Other people paint or otherwise decorate their drums in a sacred manner.

This is all a reflection of the deep relationship healers and other drummers can find in their drums. Many people find the best of themselves, the reflection and healing of their own wounds, and the means of transporting into new realities, all through the partnership with a drum.

For example, Elaine felt deeply called to find her own drum in late 1999. She looked all over the Internet and at local stores. She wondered if she should make her own drum, but worried that she wouldn't be able to "do it right." She enlisted spirit aid in helping her drum come to her. For a while, all she received was a deeper and deeper longing for her drum that she could not find.

Elaine found herself drawn to the work of one special woman who creates drums in a very unique and sacred way. Elaine e-mailed this woman to say that her guides suggested that this woman either had Elaine's drum already or was going to make it for her. Elaine asked this woman to go within and ask her guides if she did have Elaine's drum. Then Elaine turned the whole issue over to her spirit guides and the "Drummers of the Universe."

On New Year's Eve 1999, a joyful Elaine received her drum—now known as "Braveheart"—from this special drum maker. It is made of buffalo hide and, at that point, had not yet shared its name with her. The drum has a dark bruised-looking spot at its center like a healed wound. She says that when she beats the drum, out of this wounded spot emerges the most beautiful, deep, soulful resonance that is unlike anything she has ever heard—but is also exactly like she imagined her drum would sound before it came to her. It reaches into her heart and really shakes it.

At the time, Elaine was working with a therapist who invited her to take part in a special therapy group he was beginning. He thought that she could lend something valuable to the dynamic of the group.

She decided to take Braveheart to share with her therapist, since she had a private session with him first. She took Braveheart out of the bag and proceeded to tell the therapist about how Braveheart's wounds sing so sweetly when they drum.

Elaine shared with him that she was learning about how her own wounds could sing from this singing, and what a powerful force for healing lives in those wounds. He was so moved that he asked her if she would share this with the group. Of course, she did.

Elaine made no attempt to hide her feeling for Braveheart, in spite of the fact that the group largely consisted of high-powered corporate executives. She didn't even drum, explaining that Braveheart has a very deep, loud voice and heart-altering presence. She spoke to them of her experience with her own wounds and how this drum has been so healing for her. She told them everything she told the therapist.

Elaine experienced that something very special and important was conveyed in this time. She felt that her sharing was tremendously healing for everyone involved. She left the group room knowing that she was shining. Furthermore, she could see the light reflected in their faces.

Elaine was so overcome with the joy of this experience and was in such gratitude to Braveheart for bringing this healing that she questioned how she "got so lucky" to find this drum. Then the realization hit her: "Because I am loved!"

Developing a Relationship

An old African saying goes something like this: "The drum knows its owner's hands." This speaks to the sentience of the drum and the relationship between drum and drummer. To develop a truly deep partnership, it is important to play your drum regularly. The more you work together, the stronger your relationship will become and the more easily you will be able to open to the energies you bring through as a team. This is true even if your individual energies are already attuned.

As is true in any relationship, the more you come to know each other, the better you will understand each other. Over time, our energies synchronize to an automatic level. The creations of this partnership are greater than the sum of its parts. In other words, as a true team, you effect greater healing than you could as separate individuals.

In my personal experience, one's "working" drum is tuned to the energy of the drummer. It resonates with the energy field of the one who works with it most. It also appears to be the repository of wormhole-like entryways that are specific to the individual. In passing the drum on within families or to another drummer, it is important that the energetic keys be passed on along with the drum. In order to effectively use a drum for healing or journeying, one must be able to access these energies and be accepted by the spirits.

It is equally true that the more you play your drum, work with it, and dance with it, the more in tune the two of you become. It begins to feel like an extension of your Self; a means of expressing what is in your spirit and a way to communicate with All That Is. Through your relationship with the drum, you may become the doorway for Otherworldly energies to enter into this reality.

Feeding the Drum

In Yoruban and Santerian tradition, the sacred bata drums are said to have their own spirits. They are fed and honored just as the orishas— the deities—are. In other areas of the world, drummers will offer cornmeal or sacred herbs to the drum as an honoring and purification. This is often called "feeding the drum."

I do this each time I work with my drums. Not only does it strengthen the bonds of respect and honor between us, but it also assists me in attaining an altered state of consciousness. The "food" may be placed on the inside and/or outside of the drumhead. It is swished around the head for a few moments and left as an offering to the Spirits of Place.

I will often perform a smudge ceremony before drumming for a shamanic journey or workshop. At the end of the ceremony, I smudge my drum and a beater if I am using one. You may choose to use the smudge within the drum purification ceremony rather than performing a separate smudge ceremony. This choice is entirely up to you and neither is more sacred or more effective. The full smudge ceremony is outlined below for your reference.

SMUDGE CEREMONY

You will need:

- A source of purifying smoke. I recommend smudge sticks or loose herbs such as angelica, sagebrush (*Artemisia* spp.), sweetgrass, or incenses such as sandalwood and myrrh.
- Matches or a lighter. A candle is recommended for a continuing flame, especially for smudge sticks, which may be difficult to maintain smoking.
- A heat-resistant container or incense burner.
- Optional: A feather or fan.

Take a moment to center yourself. It may help to count yourself down from ten to one. Remember to breathe deeply and from the diaphragm.

Light your smudge with respect. Invite the smoke of the sacred herbs to purify your energy and this space.

Using your feather or fan to move the smoke, or carrying the smudge stick with you, offer the sacred smoke to the six directions—North, East, South, West, Earth, and Sky—and to the Great Spirit in the center, which permeates all things. Offer blessings of respect and gratitude to each of these.

Beginning at the navel, bathe yourself in the sacred and purifying smoke. Move the smoke up to your heart area, then over your head, along your back, down to your feet, and back up to your navel.

As the smoke moves along your body, feel yourself center deeply. Breathe deeply of the smoke. See your worries and tensions dissolve in the warmth as they are carried up and away by the smoke. Ask the smoke of the sacred herbs once again to purify your energy, to clear you of all limitations, and to help you become a clear and protected channel for healing energy.

Hold your drum beater in the smoke, allowing the smoke to contact all sides of the beater. See any unwanted energies release from the beater and flow up with the smoke.

Hold your drum over the smoke. See any unwanted energies release from the drum and waft up to the Creator for transformation. If your drum has one head, hold the open side in the smoke for a moment, allowing it to fill with the smoke. Turn it up and release the smoke to the Creator as a prayer that healing may flow through your partnership with the drum.

Offer the smoke once more to each of the six directions and the Creator. Give thanks to them for their presence in your life. Thank the smoke of these sacred herbs for their assistance in purifying your energy and preparing you to meet with your loved one.

Note: Some individuals and groups believe that once a smudge is burning, it should be left to burn itself out. The truth of this will depend on your beliefs and experience. In my experience, allowing something to burn for extended periods of time is not always possible or preferable. In my journeying and work with these sacred plants, I have been taught that whether I extinguish the flame or leave it to burn itself out is not important, provided my every action is made in respect and honor.

Talking Drums

Many people believe that drums were the earliest methods of communication. The djembe drum is said to be one of the oldest means of communication in Africa. It was often used to communicate over long distances, sometimes through a continuous link of drummers. Even today in some parts of Africa, drums are used to transmit messages between villages.

The bata drums are sacred to the Yoruban people of Nigeria and Benin. They were brought to Cuba during the slave trade and play a key role in the Yoruban-based traditions of that country. These double-headed drums are said to have been brought to the people by the orisha Shango, an ancient and deified king. The bata are used almost exclusively for religious purposes and can approximate the tonal qualities of the Yoruban language so well that they are called Talking Drums. They are used to recite prayers, poetry, invocations, announcements, and more.

Communication through the drum is one of the closest methods we have in this world to approximate the Otherworldly experience. Music in all forms has a way of bypassing thought and touching our emotions. When we drum, the experience is not limited by language or through translation into the symbols of this reality. It simply flows through the rhythm, and those around us are gifted with a direct glimpse into a highly personal experience.

The drum, as Portal, is frequently used to invoke beneficial energies, spirit guides, and specific deities for the work at hand. In chapter 3, I described the use of the drum in divination. I suggested developing your own "map" on the head of a drum for this purpose, but the meaning in the signs on the heads of ancient drums goes far beyond a unique divination spread.

Images and symbols for the deities and the special spirit allies of the shaman are ritually placed on the drum, whether on one or both sides of the head or along the rim. These act as smaller portals for those specific energies to come through. Often the image is created through the use of a sacred dye or the blood of the shaman. This increases the power of the placement and binds the shaman, the drum, and the spirit together.

When a spirit comes through, there is frequently an accompanying rhythm that evolves. Many cultures invoke their deities with specific rhythms. Some traditions teach a unique rhythm for each of the directions when creating sacred space.

I find this to be very similar to the Saami understanding of the *joik*. The joik is a type of singsong chanting that conveys the essence of a person, place, or thing. Joiker and joik are integral parts of the experience and they directly influence each other. Each Saami has his or her own joik, just as each human and deity has a unique rhythm. Through playing that rhythm, we evoke aspects of Self or invoke the spirits we want to work with.

Healing Rhythms

Traditionally, the drum was one of the methods available to healers for the treatment of both psychological and physical ailments. Rhythm, not always limited to drumming, has been used as a healing modality throughout the world for centuries. Our bodies and spirits synchronize with the rhythm and begin to resonate in a more harmonious way.

In modern times, many studies have been done on the therapeutic use of sound, including drumming. The ideal rhythm varies according to the researcher. Psychobiological studies have found that those in meditative and shamanic trance produce greater amounts of alpha and theta frequencies than do people in normal states of consciousness. Rhythms in these ranges are preferable for inducing trance and creating healing.

When we are in normal consciousness, our brain waves fall into the beta range, from fourteen to twenty-one cycles per second. The next level down is that of light trance in alpha. Brain waves here are in the seven to fourteen cycles per second range. Below that is the deeper trance of theta at four to seven cycles per second. The deepest levels that are normally only attained during dreaming or in comas exist at delta, below four cycles per second. These deepest levels should only be used by experienced shamans and qualified professionals.

Some healers correlate the three main sounds that may be made on many drums with the beta, alpha, and theta levels of brain activity. The deeper, bass sound often found in the center of the drum is associated with the theta level. Alpha is produced by the middle sound, about halfway back to the rim. Beta corresponds to the highest sound, sometimes the slap sound on a djembe. Not only does everyone have their own healthy rhythm, but they also need to find their own harmony with these three sounds to align all the levels of mind and body. Of course, not all drums have these three sounds and not all people resonate with this model.

It has been my experience that the best rhythm really depends on several factors, including the nature of the complaint, the area of the body affected, the individual's stage of development, and current life situation. In the hands of a skilled healer, the rhythms come through naturally, without interference from analytical thought.

The rhythm we use may vary according to the individual, the complaint, the spirits that are called upon or choose to come through, and several other factors, including simply what the healer feels is required at the time. It is not always something that can be predicted. Different rhythms create or invoke different energies. Just as the same antibiotic cannot be used to clear up every bacterial infection, so, too, do we need specific rhythms for the various conditions.

A natural rhythm exists within a healthy energy field. Most people have been aware that someone was upset or ill simply through how they felt. We may say that we didn't like the "vibes" somewhere, or it just didn't "feel" right. This is an innate recognition of these natural vibrations or rhythms.

Many healers have found that each organ and each chakra is associated with a specific rhythm. When the individual is healthy, the energy flows easily throughout the body and these rhythms interact harmoniously. When using the drum, or other sound, for healing, we restore the healthy natural rhythm to the individual system. We invigorate the energy field and return the natural harmonious flow throughout all the energy bodies.

Rhythm has also been used to alter brain-wave frequencies and synchronize the hemispheres of the brain. Some modern techniques, such as the Silva Method sound and the Hemi-Sync technology of the Monroe Institute, use a variety of sounds to accomplish this goal. Shamanic drumming serves a similar purpose.

Shamanic drumming is known as an auditory driver. This means that drumming is an auditory stimulus that entrains one's brain-wave frequencies. Simply through hearing the rhythm of the drum, we are moved into an altered state of consciousness. One's entire energy field synchronizes with the rhythm of the drum. The rattle and some forms of chanting work in similar ways.

When working with drum healing, we allow the rhythm or rhythms that are right for the person in need to come through. We listen for any change in the sound of the drum that might indicate a change in the individual's energy field. However, it is vital that we stay open to intuition and spirit guides. It is quite possible to get so caught up in listening for a tonal change that you miss something much more subtle. Sometimes the change we hear is not truly an auditory thing. It may be something we hear or feel on another level that lets us know we need to change the rhythm or stop altogether.

This intuitive listening to both the drum and your spirit guides is also important in developing your own understanding of what you are hearing and experiencing. A subtle, harmonious change may merely indicate that you are within the sphere of a new organ or chakra. Until you gain experience and allow your guides to work through you, it is possible to miss a subtle change that indicates a block or injury.

It is best to start out with a heartbeat sound or something a bit faster. This is largely a personal preference. However, the heartbeat does tend to be a good baseline from which to allow the individual rhythms to evolve. Many people will find that the higher chakras resonate best with faster rhythms, but this will depend on the complaint and the individual. You may find that you don't remember or are not consciously aware of the rhythms you play in healing sessions because your logical mind is fully shut down, enabling you to channel exactly what is required.

It is important for both healer and person in need of healing to be aware of what areas of the body-mind are affected during this process. Any unusual sensations, thoughts, feelings, and any changes to these should be noted. Each body and mind will be affected in a unique way by a specific tone or rhythm. The healer must be cautioned not to assume that what worked for one person will work for any other.

Once the areas in need of attention have been identified, the drum purification ceremony may be used, or you may prefer to incorporate drumming into any form of circle that is appropriate. During a healing session, it is often best to begin by drumming along the periphery of the body.

If you can see or feel the aura, then drum that egg-shaped energy that surrounds the physical body. If you are not yet consciously aware of this, simply drum about twelve inches out from the body beginning at the feet, going over the head, and down the other side, and then doing each side in a similar fashion. Many healers find we open the energy field by drumming from the front of the feet over the head to the back, and close it in reverse. You may want to experiment with this, perhaps opening the field at the beginning and closing it at the end of a session. If you expect this session to last longer than ten minutes, I would suggest having the person being worked on sit or lie down.

Beginning in this way will tone the general energy field and set the stage for more directed, intensive healing. At this point you may choose to work on one particular area, or the total body. Each healer develops his or her own method for this. You might experiment with holding a rhythm until you feel a need to change, or dropping your rhythm down to a heartbeat in between the general toning and the specific points. Either method will allow you to notice any slight changes, which might lead you to a point that you were unaware needed attention. One method will probably work better for you than the other.

When addressing specific points, hold the drum directly over the area as close as you feel is necessary without touching the physical body. Beginning with the heartbeat, speed up gradually until you feel you are at the correct tempo. You may choose to maintain a steady beat at this point. If you feel drawn to play more complex rhythms, trust your intuition and go with this while maintaining your focus on the healing at hand. It is quite common for the healing to require this combination in order to be most effective.

The energy of the drum may be directed through the back or bottom of the drum for healing. The rim or body of the drum has a way of funneling the sound and the energy in that direction. It is not necessary to direct the energy of the drum in this way during a healing session, however, you may feel drawn to do so in certain areas.

It is important to be aware that these may be areas in need of more intense or focused energy. Alternatively, they may be areas with excessive energy build-up that may require a funneling off of some energy. If it is not too cumbersome to do so, trust your feeling and use the open end to direct the sound.

Larger drums may also be used to effect healing, such as the ashiko and djembe. In fact, the djembe is often referred to as the "healing drum." This is generally done in two ways. The individual in need may receive healing through playing the drum alone or in a drum circle, or through non-drumming participation in a drum circle.

In *Pagan Parenting,* I write of my family's use of drumming to release emotion.[5] Our son is learning not to simply bang on the drum, since it is a sacred object to be respected. However, when we need to release stress or anger, even sadness, we will play together and allow our emotion to flow through the rhythm. In this way, we do not allow potentially destructive emotion to be repressed and build up until it causes illness or injury. This is one important way for an individual to create healing and promote health for oneself. I recommend that any healers using the drum in healing also use a drum in this way for their own clearing and healing.

There is one additional note I will make here, and that is regarding the drum overtone, sometimes called the drone or the undertone. Many types of music produce a seemingly separate sound that appears to generate on its own through the music. Often in drum circles, a musical (as opposed to percussive) sound will be heard above the drumming. Even with a single drum, an overtone can be created. These tones are useful both as healing sounds and as guiding sounds for the shamanic journey. They should be experimented with and their effects noted just as you would any rhythm.

Rituals

Historically, the drum was associated with specific rituals that created the necessary conditions for effecting a total healing. These rituals can be just as useful to us today. Unlike modern mainstream medicine, our goal is not simply to return the individual to normal

5. Madden, *Pagan Parenting,* 184.

functioning. Our goal as healers is to heal the body and spirit for more complete and long-term health. For a great many people, ritual has a deep effect on the psyche. Often, ritual alone can bring about a sufficient change in the spirit and beliefs of a person to catalyze healing.

Before doing any ritual drumming, traditional drummers often undergo a period of preparation. This is similar to the preparation most priests and priestesses go through for any ritual. It is a time of physical, mental, and spiritual preparation that includes clearing, leaving behind the mundane world, opening to Spirit, and readying the body-mind for the ritual at hand. For the ritual drummer, this also includes readying the drum.

The ritual preparation below can be incorporated into any other drumming ritual. Some people prefer to abstain from food or sex for a period of time before a ritual. Sexual abstinence is something you will need to experiment with if you choose. Some people find that the build-up of energy after a period of abstinence and the lack of any residual energy from this type of encounter is beneficial for them during drumming or any ritual. Other people find that it is easier for them to relax and release the mundane world after sexual intimacy.

Food is a very different story. If you are able to maintain your own energy level and your personal health through fasting, perhaps it is for you. I would simply caution you that solo drumming may require far less of your physical reserves than participating in a drumming circle can. If you do choose to fast for drumming rituals, be sure to have plenty of drinking water available, particularly if your ritual involves a drum circle or intense, prolonged drumming.

Before preparing for ritual, you may wish to create a special water or, for the hand drummer, a special hand ointment.[6] A recipe for each

---

6. To purchase hand ointment or drum conditioner using the recipe in this book, contact Kyanite6@aol.com.

follows. This is a general suggestion. Feel free to alter it to fit your purposes.

BLESSED WATER

If possible, use a cup of spring water, rain water, or other naturally collected water. If this is not possible, tap water is acceptable.

Take a small amount of sacred herbs, such as the ones you use in smudging, and sprinkle them over the surface of the water. Ask that the sacred herbs clear and purify this water of all unwanted energies and influences that it might be a pure channel for healing.

Hold this cup of water between your hands just above eye level. Visualize the healing you hope to achieve and send the energy through your hands and third-eye chakra into the water.

Lower the cup. Take a deep breath and hold your healing intention as you hold your breath. Release this intention to the water as you blow your breath out onto the surface of the water.

If you are working with solar or lunar energies, leave the water out in the sunlight for one full day or in the moonlight for one full cycle of the moon. Ask the spirits of land and sky to bless this water.

HAND OINTMENT

You will need:
- beeswax
- pure virgin olive oil
- essential oils, such as angelica and sandalwood
- ground herbs, such as leopard's bane/mountain tobacco (*Arnica montana*), calendula/pot marigold (*Calendula officinalis*), comfrey (*Symphytum officinale*), and witch hazel (*Haemamelis virginiana*)

- glass, stone, or pottery container
- glass, stone, or wood stirring utensil

Melt the beeswax over low heat. (The beeswax used is 10–12 percent of the volume of olive oil). When it is melted enough to be easily blended, remove it from the heat and transfer to a glass, stone, or pottery container.

Hold the essential oil bottles and then the ground herbs in both hands and send your prayers into them through your hands. This is a good time to ask for healing and protection for yourself and for those you work healing.

Add the oils and herbs to the beeswax and blend well. As you stir them into the wax, breathe your intentions into the mix. Give thanks to the herbs and your helping spirits for their blessings and protection.

Seal the container and allow it to cool.

DRUM RITUAL PREPARATION

Allow yourself some time alone with your drum before beginning any ritual. You should already have your ritual space set up with the altar and any ritual or healing tools you will need.

Wash your body and hands well. If you use blessed water or a special ointment during ritual playing, anoint yourself with this now. As you do, ask for the blessings of your deities or helping spirits in the work you are preparing to do.

Feed the drum in your usual manner, using whatever herbs or other "food" is most appropriate for your drum.

Sit in silence with your drum, focusing on your partnership, your sacred bond, and aligning your energies in harmony.

Play the drum softly and slowly until you feel you are resonating well together. Thank the drum for its role in your life and for its blessings in the work you do. Ask it to be with you again during this ritual and help you bring healing energy through to those in need.

DRUM PURIFICATION CEREMONY

Take several deep breaths and center yourself. Begin to beat the drum. In determining the speed of the beat, go with what feels right to you at the time. It is generally recommended that this be faster than a heartbeat.

Continue to beat the drum until you feel yourself center deeply and enter the trance state.

Holding the drum up and out from your body, offer its sound to each of the four directions. Then offer it to the Sky and the Earth. Then bring it back to the center again to offer it to the Creator.[†]

Continue to drum at the pace that resonates best for you along your entire body, stopping at each chakra for a few moments. Allow the sound and energy of the drum to harmonize your energy systems and clear unwanted vibrations. Hold the drum at each chakra, or any area that feels the need, drumming until you feel this area come into balance with the rest of your system.

Hold the drum out to the center once more as an offering of thanks to the Creator. Beat four times more quickly and then end with one strong beat.

[†] *Optional:* To purify the healing room, walk around the room and offer the sound to the entire space, paying particular attention to doors, windows, and any crystals or other objects that may hold energy from prior sessions.

Drum Circles

Drum circles are incredibly healing experiences for everyone involved. Arthur Hull writes that a drum circle creates a "kinesthetic, subsonic vibration that gives a rhythmic massage to everyone near it. This massage . . . positively influences the harmonious alignment of our physical cells, emotional states, and our spirits." Mr. Hull has participated in drum circles with inner-city gang members and autistic children. He has seen the healing take place in these situations.[7]

When a group of drummers comes together to share in a circle, they share much more than technical expertise. Once they open to their drums and to the group rhythms, they focus this heart opening and share their deepest selves. This can be a powerful tool for unity. People within the circle cannot hold onto their separation in the face of this potent Oneness. The walls come down and we connect with other people. This alone is a healing experience.

When two or more drummers come together for a specific healing purpose, their energy is combined to create something greater than just the individuals present. Whether the person in need is one of the drummers or is additionally present, they all receive the full force of this energy. Full participation is required, as it is in all the healing methods described in this book. This may include dancing, singing, or merely being actively present in the experience. The drummers gauge their work by the actions and responses of the person in need of healing, as well as through the input of their own spirit guides and intuitive feelings.

A lead drummer should be selected and this may or may not be the ritual leader. The lead drummer will guide the rhythms and monitor the energy of the circle, along with the ritual leader if that is a separate person. Circle drummers should be well briefed on rhythm breaks and maintaining a focus both on the healing at hand and on the guidance of the lead drummer.

---

7. Hull, *Drum Circle Spirit*, 22. © 1998 Arthur Hull, published by White Cliffs Media.

Focus is essential in a healing drum circle. The energy is of no benefit if it is scattered or if someone in the group is doing his or her own thing and showing off. Unless you have been trained in the ritual use of cultural rhythms and are playing a specific role in a traditional circle, the key here is to follow the lead drummer and support the flow of energy through the circle.

Healing Postures

Another aspect of drum healing is the use of ecstatic body and hand postures. This includes ecstatic dance. Sound—such as drumming, chanting, and the use of gongs, bells, or singing bowls—is used to drive the effects of these postures. Steady sounds at various frequencies may stimulate the peripheral nervous system and block the analytical mind. This allows us to easily and safely enter an altered state of consciousness. Ecstatic, or ritual, postures give form to the trance, much as a guided visualization might.

Specific postures may evoke specific journeys or emotions while others invoke certain spirits or energies. The stodhur utilized by many Nordic practitioners permit the individual to embody the form of a rune, thereby integrating that particular energy into the physical form. Other types of postures and hand positions function in similar ways.

Some postures need not be used for extended periods, although some regularity of practice is beneficial. Others, such as those described by Felicitas Goodman and Belinda Gore, are intended to be held for fifteen minutes or more. There is a specific energy to each posture. Certain kundalini yoga postures work on very specific glands and organs, while some of the ecstatic postures create healing or induce a journey.

If you can persuade the people you are called to heal to engage in dance or postures, this can be an immensely healing experience. However, it can be difficult to get modern people to free the body-mind enough to give themselves up to the rhythm. It is beyond the scope of this book to deal with specific postures and their effects. I recommend that you choose a book devoted to the topic that is in keeping with your traditions or feels right to you in some way. See the Recommended Reading section at the back of the book.

Drumming the Journey

The final way we use the drum to effect healing is through the facilitation of the shamanic trance. This is probably the best-known and most common use of the shamanic drum. The trance is healing in and of itself as it totally relaxes the physical body. Beyond that, we use the shamanic journey to gain healing directly from our spirit guides and to obtain valuable information to be used in our healing practices.

To drum for the journey of another is a sacred gift and can be a powerful addition to other healing techniques. It is absolutely vital that we release any ego that may be involved or any control issues we may bring to this. The goal is to become an open channel while holding the sanctity and protection of the space. The drummer facilitates the opening of the doors to healing through the rhythm of the drum. For this reason, it is also important that we clear our own energy fields before beginning the journeying ceremony. Whether we do this through the use of smudge, drumming ourselves, or another method is personal preference, provided that it is effective.

While it is true that drumming releases stress and negative emotions, the healer does not honor the process by coming to a session with issues remaining from a rotten day. These are certain to be released while others journey. Group journeying tends to have its own flavor, which often results in similar metaphors or images picked up from others in the ceremony. One's goal as the drummer is to contribute to the healing of this process for everyone, not to use it for a simple stress release.

The drummer for a journeying ceremony generally functions as the ritual leader. It is the drummer's responsibility to clear the area and the participants, to induce and facilitate the trance while monitoring the journeyers, to bring them back at an appropriate time, and to ensure that they are cleared and grounded before they leave the circle.

During the journey, the drum not only provides an auditory driver and the necessary energy for trance facilitation, but it also becomes a path or a cord to which the journeyers may return if necessary. When participants find their minds wandering or feel as though they are getting lost, they may return their awareness to the sound of the drum and either follow it back to their bodies or use it to spur a focused return to the journey.

Although plenty of drummers will spontaneously enter varying degrees of trance while drumming, the main goal is to maintain an awareness of the energy of the room and remain open to spirit guidance. We may be guided to direct the open end of the drum to one participant or one area of the room. We may be compelled to alter the rhythm or cut short the journey. If more than one journey is planned for a session, it is not uncommon for a theme or focus of the second journey to be received by the drummer during the first journey.

I often plan two journeys around a central topic for a two-hour shamanic workshop. Many times the second journey will be modified or even completely changed as the result of powerful impressions I receive while drumming for the first journey. I have learned to trust this guidance and go with the impressions. They inevitably turn out to be exactly what was needed most by a majority of participants.

The following is an outline of a basic healing journey ceremony. It may be expanded or altered to suit your particular needs. I recommend preparing for this ceremony by discussing the purpose of the journeying session in advance. Before entering the ritual space, any inexperienced participants should be briefed on the format of the ceremony and on what they may experience during a shamanic journey.

We do not want to dictate the journey. However, the basics of the shamanic Otherworlds, spirit guides, and the function of the drum should be described. New journeyers should be encouraged to use their imagination if necessary to get things moving. Modern people have become so used to guided visualizations directing their experience that when faced with nothing more leading than a drum, they can be spiritually stuck in a way. The use of imagination—even just a method of getting to the intended world and a suggestion of the tunnels or openings that may be encountered—can be a great help.

At this point, I should also bring up the topic of the Otherworlds and how we may experience them. Some writers and teachers believe that the openings must be something we know to exist in this world; they must be physically "real." These teachers may also believe that the experience of these worlds must conform to the traditional associations of the different worlds; that the Lowerworld is often experienced as Earthlike and is inhabited by ancestors or animal guides, and the Upperworld is often more celestial and is inhabited by humanoid guides. This only holds true if you believe it does, and even then your experience may vary.

The shamanic journey is highly personal. It is experienced and interpreted according to one's personal and cultural symbolism. It may be guided by whatever our guides feel we require at any given time. The individual experience may be significantly different. My main suggestion in this regard is to trust your own experience, not what someone else, including me, may teach. Learn your own symbolism and trust that whatever comes up is right for you at that time.

Along those lines, I disagree that the entry point to the Otherworlds must exist in this reality. What we are drawn to use may well exist in another reality. It is also true that through continued use, we can create this entry point as real in the Otherworld. Many people have had great success taking an imaginary hot-air balloon to the Upperworld or riding a subway to the Lowerworld. Again, I recommend going with whatever works for you.

It is a good idea to determine a specific rhythm to signal the return from the journey. Generally, we begin relatively quickly to drive the transition into trance and into the Otherworlds. As a nonintrusive journey facilitation, the beat is usually fairly slow and monotonous during the main portion of the journey. However, the rhythm or direction of the drum may change depending on the guidance received by the drummer. Then there is a sharp change in rhythm to alert the journeyers to finish up, say their good-byes, and begin to return to their bodies. Rapid drumming accompanies the return trip, similar to the entry. It is important that everyone is clear on the signal to return before entering the journey.

A HEALING JOURNEY

Begin with either the drum purification ceremony or the smudge ceremony.

Offer smudge or sacred herbs to the spirit of the drum. If you offer the smoke of the smudge, release this smoke to the Great Spirit. If herbs are offered to the drum, offer them to the Spirits of Place or set them aside to be offered to the spirits later.

Verify that the intent and return signal are clear to everyone.

Ask for the blessings of the Spirits of Place and the guides of all involved. Request that you and your drum be used to channel healing energy for the highest good of all concerned.

Drum the journey as described above.

As the drummer and ceremonial leader, you must maintain an awareness of the room energy and the responses of the journeyers. Direct the sound of the drum as needed. Be prepared to end the journey early if necessary.

At a predetermined amount of time, or when you feel it is time to return, give the signal and drum everyone back to the room.

When you have finished drumming, allow each person enough time to fully return to consciousness and open their eyes to the room. Maintain an awareness of the group energy and direct silence or discussion accordingly.

Thank the Spirits of Place and the spirit guides in attendance for their blessings and allow participants to offer specific thanks as they wish.

Conduct discussions in the sanctity and safety of the circle.

Thank the spirits of the directions for their protection and gifts during this ceremony.

Close the circle in your preferred manner.

It is certainly possible to drum for your own journey. Shamans have done this for millennia, although some cultures have shamanic assistants to drum, rattle, or chant while the shaman journeys. To do it for yourself does take a bit of practice. Obviously, there will be a break in the rhythm once you enter deep trance and your body relaxes beyond the point of standing or sitting, let alone drumming. Either of these occurrences may jolt you out of trance.

In general, you should begin to drum while sitting or lying down; or where you have a soft place to fall nearby. While the transition is fairly smooth and easy for most people, some people find that their trance deepens rapidly beyond the point of physical control. I do know people who will immediately fall to the ground once a deep trance is induced.

In addition, you need to be experienced in returning on your own. It is extremely rare for someone to get lost or be unable to return to the body, but it does happen. It is always best to gain experience first and have a back-up plan (let someone know what you are doing and when you expect to be finished), in case you have some difficulty.

For many shamans and most drummers, the drum is a best friend; a partner at the deepest possible level of being. Most of us develop bonds with our working drums, just as we do with other people or animals in our lives. The drum is one of the most underrated and underused tools for a healer. Begin to develop a relationship with the drum, and you are likely to find that this is a potent and highly sacred experience to which few others can compare.

7

DIVINE INSPIRATION

How many times have you seen a painting or sculpture or heard a piece of music that gave you goosebumps or brought you to tears? It seemed to reach into your heart and soul and strike a chord deep within you. These creations were truly inspired and something in you resonated with them. We are in awe of the artisans who craft such works. Their ability to bring that divine inspiration into the manifest world is amazing. Yet the simple process of opening to this and creating without judgment can be equally inspired and healing for all of us.

When we open to the Otherworlds and our own spirit guides, our lives are forever changed. Even if we are not using this connection in service to a community yet, creativity is inevitably increased through our travels beyond this realm. One of the ways this creativity comes through is in various art forms, especially music, writing, painting, and sculpture.

Historically, shamans have worked with their spirit guides and served their communities through specialized art forms. Mask-making, the creation of shields and drums, ritual jewelry, body art, and varied musical forms have been used to manifest this Otherworldly guidance in our reality. Many people find that their connection to spirit guides is strengthened when they work with the energy of guides in a tangible manner.

The use of shamanic creativity may be particularly useful to healers, not only for personal benefit but for that of those they are called to heal as well. Art and music bypass the rational mind and speak to our spirits, just as ritual and shamanic journeying do. Our creations also give us clues into the shadow side, allowing insights beyond consciousness that can increase the effectiveness of the healing process.

In recent years, art and music have become respected methods within modern mainstream therapies, just as they have been for millennia among native peoples. Today, these methods are possibly even more applicable because modern society has become so far removed from the free flow of our own creativity. We are an analytical culture, yet those shadow aspects that contribute to our suffering are very capable of eluding direct analysis.

As I will discuss in the next chapter, shadow aspects can be tricky. On one hand, they crave recognition and continue to attract situations to us that will mirror their presence within. However, they are called shadow aspects for a very good reason. They are not readily apparent, nor are they generally found on the surface of consciousness. They exist in twilight, often appearing as symbols, and they may need to be teased or tricked out of the shadows.

The wonderful benefit to the use of concrete creativity—such as is found in art and music—lies in the same unconscious connection to spirit as is found with shadow aspects. The wellspring of divine inspiration has its source deep within, where we easily communicate with spirit guides and where we can access all the multiversal knowledge that exists.

When we create, we tap into that spring and often find clues to cures within our creations. The process of creating sets the personality aside, permitting what needs to come through to manifest. I know that when I write, I will sometimes reread a chapter and wonder who really wrote it. Often I will sit in front of my computer and type, trusting that my spirit guides will take over from there. The same process evolves through the use of creativity in healing, whether you create through sculpture, poetry, song, or dance.

Creating from Spirit

The first step in using creativity is to release all judgment, embarrassment, and fear you may have regarding your ability. The goal is not the end result or the final creation. The goal is the process itself. If you have never worked with art before, it may take some experimentation to find the right form for you.

When I started as a Bard in the Order of Bards, Ovates, and Druids, I tried just about every art form. Some were things like painting and drawing that truly amaze me when I view the work of others, but these methods did not hold any spark for me. Although some of my trance creations are rather good, neither the end result nor the process really inspired me. So I tried other things and finally found those methods that work for me.

It is best to begin with something you feel drawn to, something that intrigues and excites you. The hardest part is making those first few steps: drawing the first lines, beginning to mold the clay, making the first cuts in a piece of wood or stone. Once you make that first step, you make another, then another, and before you know it you are creating.

If you tend to be a healer with an ability to use symbolism as a focal point to allow your intuition to come forth, the Scribble exercise below may work quite well for you. Even if your strength does not lie in this area, the designs that result from this exercise can be taken into the shamanic journey by just about anyone to great success. This is an exercise for healer to do together with those they work to heal. The only materials needed are colored drawing utensils and a big sheet of paper, at least legal size.

SCRIBBLE

Each person chooses a colored marker, pencil, or crayon.

The healer begins with freeform drawing on the paper. This does not need to take any form or follow any method, just scribble in any way you feel.

The person in need follows the healer and adds his or her own scribbles and detailing to the paper. It is perfectly acceptable to take turns or continue to scribble together until you both feel your Scribble is complete.

Sometimes the Scribbles will be obvious in their meanings. Frequently, we need to decipher them. The technique described in chapter 3 for scrying with clouds and rocks is quite applicable here. This type of scrying allows our spirit guides to present us with images that are meaningful. It also permits our own shadow sides to bring thoughts and images into everyday reality from just below the surface of consciousness.

A stream-of-consciousness exchange between healer and person in need of healing generally works well with the Scribble exercise. Each person begins to describe what he or she sees in the drawing. The healer makes notes of the images and ideas. Any feeling of "Ah-ha!" for either individual is noted and explored further. This is best followed up with a shamanic journey undertaken by the healer on behalf of the person in need. The image of the Scribble is held in the mind as the healer enters the journey, just as we would hold a goal or question.

Below you'll find another exercise, the Junk Walk. I first wrote about the Junk Walk in *Shamanic Guide to Death and Dying.*[1] I dis-

---

1. Madden, *Shamanic Guide to Death and Dying,* 164–65.

cussed its great benefit with children and described how I went out on a Walk with my mother, having a few personal issues in mind to work on. As I walked, I collected objects that drew my attention in a unique way. When we returned from the Walk, we sat down to create a therapeutic sculpture. I tried several things but nothing seemed to flow for the issues I was currently working on.

Then I found an old piece of metal that reminded me of a ladder. Suddenly, my mind was flooded with all the symbolism of my shamanic journey to assist my grandfather to the next world after his death. In that journey, we climbed a staircase together and this metal ladder was a powerful reminder of that experience. I had not realized that I held some lingering attachments to his death and this simple exercise facilitated the final clearing for me. I still have that ladder sculpture on my desk. It continues to inspire and intrigue me.

The Junk Walk is a process of creating multimedia sculpture that utilizes found items and leftover scraps you may have lying around. It is not necessary to begin your Walk with a specific condition in mind, although this can be beneficial in healing work. However, it is true that whatever issues need manifestation most at the time of the Walk are likely to come through, even if they are not your main focus. Trust that what comes up is right for you at the time.

JUNK WALK

Begin by standing and centering through the breath or through the senses (see chapter 10). Meditate for a moment on the concern or question at hand. Ask your spirit guides, and those of the person in need of healing if you are Walking for another person, to lead you to the right items and assist you in finding the answer through this process.

Take along a bag or box and pick up anything that draws your interest, provided it is not on private property, does not belong to someone else, and does not involve harming any living being. Pick up small items, such as feathers, pieces of paper or metal, wood chips, and so on. Also, keep an eye out for larger items that may serve as a base for your sculpture. Bring it all home from your Junk Walk.

Have things like glue, tape, string, clay, and wire ready at home. When you return from your walk, dump everything out onto a big table or the floor. Then allow yourself to create. Experiment and play. Feel free to rip something apart if it doesn't work and start over.

With time and an open mind, you will be able to create a sculpture that offers clues to the answer you seek. For the people you are called to heal, it will be a concrete means of releasing their emotions and obtaining insight into their own healing. I highly recommend this procedure for anyone involved in the healing process. This is perhaps one of the easiest and best methods for actively involving people in the healing team.

Mask-making

The use of the shamanic mask is possibly one of the oldest forms of shapeshifting and ritual art. It is also extremely beneficial as a healing tool. A mask can help the healer embody healing allies in times of need. The healer can also create a specific mask, usually received during the shamanic journey. This mask may also be worn during future journeys for the healing at hand.

As a tool for healing, the mask can effectively be used in a variety of ways. Healers should consider adding this process to their own toolkit and including it as one of the partnership techniques they suggest. The possibilities are only limited by your inspiration and imagination.

The mask can serve to externalize feelings, identities, illnesses, and behaviors that the individual in need is not fully aware of or is repressing. Simply through the creation and wearing of the mask, these issues are brought out into the light of day where they can be handled. This externalization allows this type of situation to be dealt with in a less personal way. The current identity, not the core or spirit of the individual exhibits these symptoms. This has a way of putting things in perspective, and making them appear manageable.

In order to make a mask, it is important to decide on the purpose in advance. Certainly, we allow for the mask to develop in the process and we recognize that the end result may be far from what we initially envision, but we need to have a place to begin and a focus for its creation.

This may be determined in a very individual way through dreaming or journeying. It may be something that healer and person in need uncover together through talking or by using some of the exercises in this book, such as Scribble. This is also an excellent time to use your divination methods or your pendulum.

Once the intent is established, a ceremony of mask-making can be held. It is a good idea to include some type of ritual preparation, such as the Preparatory Movement Meditation in chapter 2, a short period of exercise, or one of the purification methods in chapter 6. This preparation can be an important factor in clearing the mind and focusing the energy.

Set up your ritual as usual, having all necessary items for the creation of your mask within the ritual space. Masks may be constructed out of any material, even paper bags and magic markers. Collect anything you feel you may want to use.

Consecrate your sacred space in your preferred manner. During your invocation, be sure to invite any spirits involved in the creation or expected use of this mask. Bear in mind that you may end up evoking lost soul fragments or shadow aspects. As a result, you may also want to be prepared for an emotional release during the ceremony. Having a box of tissues on hand is highly recommended.

Depending on your relationship with the person you are working with and how the focus of the mask was determined, you may want to begin with some sharing and storytelling in this safe space. Alternatively, you may choose a guided meditation to narrow the focus and encourage the flow of inspiration. To have healer and person in need create masks together may take some of the performance pressure off one or the other, but this is certainly optional.

Allow for the mask-making to be as lighthearted or serious as it needs to be. As the healer, your job is to encourage and support the flow of healing energy throughout the rite. Provide enough time to discard and re-create as necessary, but do not permit the focus to get stuck on the aesthetics of the end result. The process is at least as important as how the mask looks.

Once the mask is complete, it should be dedicated to the healing goal and worn for a meditation, journey, or dance. This is likely to add depth and power to the experience. The journey return may take slightly longer than normal, or the wearer of the mask may prefer silence for a time after returning from the journey. However, discussion or journaling can be an essential part of understanding, integrating, and manifesting the experience.

Once your ceremony is concluded, you have two options for the handling of the mask. The wearer may choose to keep it as a reminder and focus for further work, to be ritually disposed of when health is regained. This is by far the most common choice. Alternatively, you may prefer to ritually burn the mask at the conclusion of this ceremony, releasing the energy and prayers to the multiverse for manifestation.

Singing the Spirit

The use of voice in shamanic healing is probably more common than even the use of the drum. Otherworldly music and shamanic power songs have been described in nearly all cultures around the world.

Vocal sound is used to induce and carry the trance, evoke power, bind energies, communicate Otherworldly experience, and to heal.

Druids went through extensive training in the Bardic Schools to effectively use the voice in song, storytelling, and magick. The power of the spoken word was revered among the ancient Celts. Through this great vocal ability, druids could stop battles, lay curses, and cast a variety of spells. It is believed that many of the Celtic musicians learned their craft from the Faery Folk. Whether or not this is true, it speaks to our innate recognition of the power of music and its ability to transport us beyond this realm.

Many cultures and magickal traditions believe that the spirits do not communicate as we do, and therefore are not interested in our everyday manner of speaking. In order to communicate with them we must use an extraordinary method. Song, chant, intonation, and poetry are some of the more common "extraordinary" methods we have available to us.

Communication with Otherworldly beings is the most basic use of the shamanic voice. Many of those on the shamanic path have learned to dance their power animals as a way of merging and honoring these beings. Dance is important in our society because we have become so rigid and inhibited in our normal movements. Dance can free the energy we repress in our daily lives. Song is commonly a part of this dance. Later in this chapter I offer a simple exercise to assist you in singing your own spirit guides. This need not be limited to power animals.

For the Saami, the joik plays a large part in connections with various helping spirits. Traditionally, these spirits will come upon a Saami youth and joik a special song. The next day, the young Saami returns to that same place. If the spirit chooses to work with this individual, it also returns for two more days and repeats the same joik. The young Saami must joik the same song each day in order to keep this spirit. From that point on, this spirit will come to that Saami whenever their special song is joiked.

The goal of this exercise is to open yourself to direct communication with any spirit guide. This exercise will not only allow you to sing the song you share with this guide, but it will enhance your ability to hear and understand when they have messages for you. If you feel uncomfortable about this type of exercise, you may choose to practice with the Finding Your Voice exercise that follows before undertaking any of the other exercises in this chapter.

SINGING YOUR SPIRIT GUIDES

Enter the shamanic trance by your usual method. If you prefer, you may count yourself down from ten to one, stopping periodically to take a deep breath and remind yourself to go deeper.

While in your meditative trance state, call upon your main spirit guide, even if you do not yet know who or what this being is. Ask that you may be given a special song to share with this guide. Let it be known that your voice is open to the energy of your partnership and that you desire to merge with this being at this time.

Take a deep breath and release any embarrassments, judgments, or other limitations and allow yourself to sing whatever comes to mind. You may find yourself simply toning. You may sing a wordless melody or one with animal sounds. Your song may take the form of a monotonous chant, which may or may not rhyme. Trust whatever comes up as right for you at this time and go with it. See where it leads.

When you feel you have experienced what you set out to do, or that your song is complete for now, thank your guide for sharing this with you. Thank this guide for all the assistance and blessings it brings you each day. Promise not to forget and to return to work with this guide again.

Return to normal consciousness and keep your promises. If you counted yourself down, repeat the process in reverse to count yourself back up.

In modern society, we lose this ability to naturally use the voice. Unless we are small children or trained performers, many of us have blocks in our throat chakras from a need to communicate only in acceptable ways geared to specific situations. We grow up to be rather rigid, feeling ridiculous dancing or singing freely. This effectively blocks true creativity. It limits our ability to communicate honestly and to be open to the Otherworlds.

The exercise below is designed for modern people in just this situation. I highly recommend it for anyone, but particularly for those who will not sing in public and even feel embarrassed about their ability to carry a tune in private. Use some of your time alone to work with this exercise regularly. Allow your spirit to soar as you joyfully express yourself without any thought to how you look or sound.

This exercise is designed as a process of steps to be taken over a period of time. This is not a usual exercise where each step is to be done immediately after the previous step. Work with each step for a matter of days or months, however long you need. Move on to the next step only when you feel comfortable with the one you have been working.

FINDING YOUR VOICE

Begin by simply humming a tone to yourself while you are alone. Listen to the tone without judgment and allow it to find its own pitch. Feel your head and throat vibrate with the sound.

When you feel comfortable with humming, begin to use simple chants while you are alone in a safe space. "Om" or "Awen" (pronounced *ah-oo-en*) are ideal beginning tones to chant. Feel your body vibrate with the tone.

Again in a safe space where no one can hear you, begin to hum or chant whatever sounds or combination of sounds you feel. Allow your voice to take over as it will and give yourself freely to the sound without judgment.

Make up a simple song about yourself, your goals, your guides, and your dreams of where the shamanic path will lead you. Sing it as loud as you like and really have fun with it. Allow it to create its own energy as you channel your personal energy through the song.

Shamans across the world have traditionally used special power songs. Often the melodies were traditional while the words were specific to the shaman. These are generally slow and monotonous, much like shamanic drumming, and they are frequently used to induce trance states. Power songs are also used for healing, to commune with spirit guides, and to raise the energy of sacred sites.

As healers, we use power songs to open to spirit guidance and to infuse ourselves with the energy we will need for healing. The personality that we currently hold steps out of the way as the power song begins the process of funneling this healing energy through us into the session and the person in need. Once you have evoked and merged with your power song, you may call it up whenever you need. It may change as you do, but it will forever be a part of you.

SEEKING YOUR POWER SONG

Find a place where you feel safe and are unlikely to be disturbed. If possible, choose a place in Nature. Wander around to get a feel for this place.

Make an offering of thanks, and perhaps sacred herbs or water, to the spirits of this place and to the Creator. Ask for their blessings and protection in this work that you are about to do.

Enter the shamanic trance by your usual method. If you prefer, you may count yourself down from ten to one, stopping periodically to take a deep breath and remind yourself to go deeper.

While in your meditative trance state, go deep within your Self. Find who you are at your core, beyond your identity and the roles you play in this world. Feel yourself embodying the True You as you are filled with the energy of the multiverse. You are open to healing energy and to communication with spirit guides.

Begin to sing from this place of vitality, honesty, and power. Allow all you feel and all that you are to flow into your song. Be aware of any changes in your energy or body as the song becomes part of your being.

When you feel you have experienced what you set out to do, or that your song is complete for now, give thanks to all those that walk with you, guide you, and enliven you. Sit in silence for a moment and take note of how you feel. Then return to normal consciousness.

Chanting

Mantras and chanting have been used in many areas of the world for self-healing, spiritual growth, and to heal others. Tibetan shamans believe the use of mantra heals certain types of sickness and can even increase the effectiveness of medications. Like drumming, chanting can entrain the body-mind, bringing all aspects of Self into harmony with the chant and releasing energy blockages.

In chapter 6, I wrote about finding the correct rhythm for the individual and the specific healing need. The healing process is similar when vocal sound is used in place of the drum. Each person has a unique tone that resonates them into balance and health. Each individual complaint has a corresponding tone that will effect change and bring about healing. Often the tone will be felt at the base of the skull, just above the neck. It will vibrate there and the person will feel more relaxed and more centered than before.

Chanting or toning is created through more than the mouth and throat. Its resonation is felt throughout the head and body. Some healers will use well-known Eastern mantras, such as "Om." Some will chant the names of deities or spirit guides, or simply beneficial words like "Balance" and "Harmony." Others try to remain within the framework of the shamanic tradition they follow. For example, seidr (Norse) practitioners may chant the runes.

Earlier I described the piezoelectric properties of quartz crystals that allow these crystals to convert mechanical vibrations, such as sound and pressure, into electrical signals. This means that striking a crystal will produce an electrical effect that can be used in healing, much like ultrasound is used. These electrical effects create a similar resonance in the body that healing energy work can. In Qi Gong, a Chinese healing system, flat pieces of jade known as *singing stones* are struck for their healing resonance. When placed on the body at areas of concern or within the energy field, these effects can entrain the body-mind into harmony.

Sound is another mechanical vibration that can induce an electric signal in piezoelectric crystals, such as tourmaline and quartz. A crystal or a thin slab of crystal is placed on the areas of concern or on each chakra point. These may also be placed within the energy field of the person in need of healing, either around the body or at the head and feet. The healer may then intone a specific chant that causes the crystals to resonate, bringing the energy of the person in need into alignment and releasing blocks or unhealthy energies.

This is one of those partnership techniques that can be taught to those with whom a healer is called to work. The healer should journey to find the correct chant or mantra for the individual in need. Teach the person you are working with to intone the mantra while holding the appropriate crystal, and ask him or her to remain aware but unattached to any area of the mind or body where a change is felt. These areas and feelings can then be discussed with the healer at the next session.

Incantations

Shamans and sorcerers have used incantations for millennia to invoke the spirits and to bind specific energies. The use of incantations in spellwork crosses all traditions. Your spirit guide song and your power song may be considered to be types of incantation as well.

The incantation as healing spell was largely a secret held only by traditional healers. To tell the uninitiated the incantation formula was to dilute its power and effectiveness. Often the incantation could only be uttered during a healing session. In and of itself, the incantation was a healing act. However, it was frequently accompanied by the use of magickal gestures, healing herbs, and the magickal use of crystals and the breath.

Because of the magickal intent, incantations generally take the form of toning or monotonous chanting. Within the chant, there are usually certain words that you will use to carry the force of your intent. These may be names of deities, or action words calling an illness out from the person in need and into an object. These words should be intoned, much like one might chant a mantra like "Om."

This intonation is generally preceded by a deep breath. As you exhale, you send the intent of this incantation out with the intonation. You will feel your throat, head, then your body, and then the energy of the area begin to vibrate with this sound. As you project the tone, you project the thought and emotion.

The use of breath is important when creating incantations. Many cultures believe that the will or goal is carried on the breath. This is a similar concept to that of the Native American pipe. The smoke is the breath of the Creator, and our prayers are carried to this Great Spirit on the breath and the smoke. Therefore, it is just as important to blow the thought out into the multiverse or onto the specific object as it is to vibrate your words.

There is no definite rule of how to create effective incantations. You must find what works best for you through practice and experimentation. At least in the beginning, it is generally best to keep it simple and short. Repetitive phrases help you to remember what you need to chant and reinforce the will behind the words.

The use of song in shamanic practice has been avoided and underrated in recent years. We feel more comfortable drumming or rattling or listening to a tape than we do chanting or singing. Whether you seek your own power song, use healing incantations, or just hum to yourself on the way home from work, I encourage you to experiment with freeing your voice.

Songlines are tracks across the Australian landscape created by the aboriginal ancestors when they sang the land into existence from their home in the Dreamtime. These have been compared to leylines or vortex points—places of Earth power. These aboriginal people keep ceremonial songs, which pass on these stories and allow them to follow the Songlines.

Freeing your creativity can open your access to a similar type of Songline. Whether you use voice or material art, this practice opens a doorway to more than your inner Self. It connects you with the Land, the Ancestors, and the Spirit World. It permits renewed access to Dreaming and helps you manifest your goals.

As you reactivate your heart and throat, your creativity will be enhanced. The energy in your body and your life will flow more freely, bringing you insights and abundance. You may be surprised at the healing you observe in your own life, simply through reconnecting with your manifestation of the Divine Inspiration. The benefit to your healing work is likely to amaze you.

8

INTO THE SHADOWS

Deeper and deeper I went, moving into my own inner Self.
Darkness surrounded me. The walls of my tunnel were made
of images flying toward me and then past me as I slid along. I
rode this tunnel down along a current of tension and watched
as the images showed me parts of myself I had not looked at
for some time. I saw fears, embarrassments, experiences, and
people. I saw odd symbols that, at face value, seemed to make
no sense and yet there was an emotional charge to each of
them. Then I could hear them as well, voices from my shadow
reminding me of things I have denied. The voices seemed
much louder and harsher, as if they had grown in an echo
chamber while I was away.

This is an excerpt from my 1996 journal. It relates a little of an
incredible and spontaneous journey that a spirit guide gave me no
choice about embarking upon. In the year leading up to this, I had
consciously repressed some very emotional and traumatic experiences.
This journey brought me face to face with these soul fragments and
blocked chakras. It is one of the most powerful journeys I have ever
experienced. Although I have consciously done some truly intense

work on remaining shadows since then, I can say that this forced exploration of my shadow side was life-changing.

Many of those on a shamanic path speak of the shadow side, yet this aspect of Self is not well covered in shamanic literature. Some books do not deal with it at all. Perhaps this is because a balance between light and dark is inherent in the shamanic path. However, most of those coming to shamanism in modern times were not raised with this understanding. Some people who have come through other channels may be completely focused on projecting a good and loving persona.

There is nothing wrong with being "good" and loving if it is honest, but even those of us who feel that way much of the time do not feel that way all the time. We deserve to honor all of who we are. It is for this reason that I have devoted an entire chapter to the Shadow Side. Anyone working with magick, trance states, healing, or shamanism needs to understand how the shadow works in our lives and our trances.

What do we really know of our shadows? We may have a rational understanding of the shadow side as the repository of our fears, destructive patterns, soul fragments, limitations, and so on. We may perceive this to be the subconscious. We may believe these aspects of Self to reside somewhere in the Otherworlds, in our chakras, or within various body parts. No matter what you believe, what direct experience do you really have of your own shadow side?

Do you seek it out for exploration or avoid it? Do you get to a certain degree of discomfort and stop there? Do you focus on white light and being a "nice" person, or do you actively attempt to integrate your own dark side? Take a moment to consider how you react to these feelings, memories, and reactions when they come up. Reflect on the people that come to you for healing. Are they mirroring something within you that you refuse to see? Think about whether or not these are things that you readily share with the people in your life.

The exercise below is designed to evoke all your beliefs and associations surrounding shadow aspects. Once the initial exercise is performed with the word *Shadow,* you should come back to this exercise and use specific shadow elements as the word of origin. You may be surprised at where they lead you and the clues to healing and integration this exercise can offer.

SHADOW ASSOCIATION WEB EXERCISE

Write the word *Shadow* in the center of a clean sheet of paper.

Write down any words that come to mind when you think about the word *Shadow.* You may do this in linear fashion from left to right, or you may feel drawn to place certain words in different areas of the paper.

Draw lines connecting each word to its source word. If a word comes up that sparks another association, go with that flow and connect each word to the word it arose from. When that line has played out or appears to go off on an unrelated tangent, return to the word *Shadow* and begin again.

Thanks to some religions and *Star Wars,* the dark side has come to symbolize Evil. The dark side has been labeled as all that we do and rightly should fear. When repressed and denied, the shadow can act like something "evil." It will create and attract situations that force us to see it in the reflection of our experience. It causes us to have moments of behavior that frighten or frustrate us. These are those fits of word and action that we can't believe came from us. It must have been the alcohol, or the anger, or because someone just pushed us too far. In these situations, the shadow erupts in a flash and then just as quickly retreats back into the darkness.

When we decide to do trance work for personal benefit or for the healing of other people, we need to learn our personal symbolism.

We also need to develop the ability to determine what is real and what is imagined. Many people in the beginning stages of journeying and meditation feel that they are making things up in trance. This may even occur during hypnosis sessions.

Early on, it doesn't matter if we are making things up. We are working through our own doubts as well as through the initial layer of stuff that has accumulated in our consciousness. As that gets cleared out, we begin to believe that our experiences arise from somewhere outside of us. We look to these journeys for messages from spirit guides and as actual out-of-body encounters. When the shadow is still interfering without our awareness, these experiences may simply be more of what we encountered in the early stages of trance work.

The shadow side may be seen as the unconscious, or subconscious, to use psychological terms. Freud was the first one to really identify this process of submerging unwanted aspects of Self and repressing them. He was also the one to term this process *projection,* although the concept had been around for ages. Repression is seen as the first line of defense against unwanted impulses, according to psychoanalytic theory. In this system, projection is just one of several mechanisms that arise from repression.

C. G. Jung, who originally coined the term *shadow,* took this one step further. He believed that repression necessarily leads to projection. To Jung, projection was more than the externalization of undesirable, and usually sexual, attributes and impulses that have been repressed. He defined it as the projecting and mirroring in external situations and other people of anything that does not resonate with the current ego identification. This may include positive qualities that we are not ready to assimilate. Therefore, projection is necessary for integration to occur.

This concept is found in many other modern fields of psychology. Fritz Perls of the Gestalt school said that our eyes are not windows but mirrors. According to these dualist theories, we do not just happen upon these mirrors, we actively seek them out, although perhaps not consciously.

According to the Vedantic school of thought, the universe exists so that we can experience it, and in doing so, become liberated and whole. This idea is found throughout the Yoga Sutras and the Upanishads. What is without is within; the macrocosm is the microcosm. The concept of karma is applicable here as well.

Karma is not what it has come to mean in common New Age belief. It is not a system of cause and effect that we experience as reward or punishment. The goal is to create balance and integration. According to the original understanding of karma, experience manifests as *samskaras*. These are like layers of experience, often taking the form of what shamans refer to as soul fragments. These samskaras can group together, creating external situations that mirror our internal shadows.

For the healer, the shadow is of great importance. First and foremost, we need to continue to work on our own shadows in order to effectively heal. The clearer the healer is in his or her Self, the more accurate the healer will be and the more easily he or she will be able to channel pure healing energy to a person in need. While many of us do attract individuals who teach us about our own Stuff, healers who deny personal shadows will tend to project these issues onto the people they work with, making diagnoses questionable.

I knew a man several years ago who believed he was one of the great healers of our time. He was quite good and many people benefited from his work, particularly his knowledge of herbs. He was a Wiccan high priest and had gone through all the necessary training and initiations. As a result, he was certain that he had cleared all his stuff and really knew himself well. The thing was that he saw very similar issues in everyone he encountered.

This man found egocentrism everywhere he went. Many of his relationships ended because he felt the other people were just too wrapped up in themselves. His healing sessions almost always ended with the suggestion that his clients do more work on themselves and give up some of their ego. Unfortunately, he did more harm than good on occasion because of this.

He refused to entertain the possibility that he might be projecting. He said that those who suggested it were simply jealous of his incredible ability and growing celebrity. In doing so, he blocked healing in his own life, and his counsel was often not what was really required by his clients.

This is certainly an extreme case, but it illustrates the point well. The clearer we get, the better we heal.

Healers also need to be aware of the impact of the shadow on the people we are called to heal. This can be the cause of many recurring or undiagnosable (by modern medical methods) illnesses and conditions. It can give rise to unhealthy or unwanted behaviors. Shadow issues can block or impair healing. Lack of trust and belief in the healer may also spring from fears and old beliefs that remain in the shadow side. Again, as shamanic healers, treating the whole person is vital to success.

While it is commonly understood that mental conditions and life patterns often spring from the shadow side, it is equally true that many physical issues also have their origins here. I suffered a serious back injury after college that was the direct result of my own shadow aspects. It was as though several of my samskaras banded together to activate and knock me out for a time of badly needed reflection and personal work.

I have a friend who used to get deathly ill whenever he was called to care for someone else or do something that he felt was inconvenient. This could obviously be attributed to stress, and most psychologists would point out that this was an avoidance tactic, but it was his shadow aspects that were the source of this significant stress.

Through a combination of exercises over a period of almost one year, my friend was able to handle his reactions and prevent himself from falling ill. In retrieving power animals, he regained the strength necessary to say no when it was appropriate. Through finding his power song and reconnecting with spirit guides, he found ways of maintaining his personal power through situations that he could not avoid. Also, through the use of shamanic journeying and several of the exercises outlined in this book, he was able to re-experience and reintegrate his own lost soul fragments.

The following exercise, Walk for At-one-ment, is adapted from a course called Avatar, specifically from the ReSurfacing workbook.[1] It may seem simplistic and rather nonshamanic at first. However, it is an excellent method for getting in touch with your own shadows and releasing emotions. It truly becomes more effective with practice and a willingness to be vulnerable to your Self. I have used it with great success to free my own trapped soul fragments.

You should know that once you have released your resistance, you might find that certain issues may give rise to very long Walks. You may also be led off on what may initially appear to be completely separate issues. I recall one Walk that I started out on to clear my frustrations from my work in a laboratory. I ended up walking for two hours, crying and yelling about things from my childhood that suddenly all seemed clearly connected. It was a surprisingly intense and freeing experience.

WALK FOR AT-ONE-MENT

1. To begin, choose a direction. If possible, perform this exercise out in the wilderness, up a mountain trail, or up a flight of stairs. It is preferable to do this in a space where you feel safe and able to freely express your feelings.

2. Begin walking in your chosen direction and with each step, whisper an action you have done or a thought or intention you have had that was motivated by fear or

---

1. Page 61, Avatar® materials by Harry Palmer. Excerpted with permission by Harry Palmer © 2000. Avatar® and ReSurfacing® are registered trademarks of Star's Edge, Inc.

anger. Include any act you are reluctant to express or for which you feel guilt; any act for which you have a justifying belief or for which you feel a need to explain. Also include any nonactions when you really should have acted.

3. Allow yourself to fully experience anything that may come up. With each step, move forward with another action, thought, or intention.

4. When you feel you are ready to end this exercise, or feel that you have cleared all that is needed at this time, take some time and contemplate *spans of time.*

5. With every step on your return, think of someone and whisper, "May you be blessed with joy and health."

6. Release all thoughts and events to the past, and experience the sights, sounds, and sensations of the present moment with appreciation.

Variations

1. *For self-abasement:*
   - Use self-criticisms for step 2 and "May I be blessed with joy and health" for step 5.
   - Follow this exercise with criticism of others for step 2 and "okay" to something for step 5.

2. *For any period of time right before you made (or are about to make) a major change in your life:*
   - Use something you were/are trying to keep secret for step 2 and something you could reveal for step 5.

The following is a meditation that developed out of my own journeys to my center. Its goal is similar to that of the Walk for At-one-ment. When I made the decision to finally complete this book, I set out to really explore my shadow side. Many of those journeys assumed a similar framework that I used as the basis for this meditation. I have offered this at workshops around the country and other people have found it to be so powerful for them that I include it here for your use. It is written as a guided meditation and you may want to tape record it to listen to later on. It is designed for use with an optional shamanic drumming tape, but alternatively, you may follow your breath. Please allow for plenty of undisturbed time in a safe, comfortable space whenever you perform this meditation.

THROUGH THE SHADOW MEDITATION

Allow the drumming to carry you down, deep within yourself. Follow the sound of the drum as it resonates with your own energy. Ride this tunnel of sound into the center of your being.

Deep within your center, you see a dark doorway. Ride the sound of the drum through this doorway and into the deep darkness beyond. Become aware of your spirit guides surrounding you in safety and comfort as you move deep into the darkness.

As you follow the sound of the drum, images come forth out of the darkness and pass by you. Recognize these as events and people from your own life. Some may show up as symbols of your own beliefs and experiences. It is possible that a few of them may not appear to be based in this lifetime and may be the result of past-life experiences. Watch them without judgment as you move beyond them. Soon all you see is the darkness.

Now you find yourself at your core. Your guides are right there with you standing in absolute darkness. Call forth one image from the darkness. Ask that this be an image that holds a minor emotional charge and allow it to approach you.

Take a good look at this image. What meaning does it hold for you? What can you learn from its presence in your life? Why do you fear it? Be aware of any communication from your guides during this process.

Now reach out and embrace this image with acceptance. Acknowledge this as a part of you that has been denied. Feel yourself become more complete as you integrate this experience. Now take a deep breath and blow all the feelings and judgments you have attached to this thing into a bubble of shadow. Take another deep breath and feel them leave your body as you blow them out into the bubble.

The bubble is filling with light. It is expanding and transforming these feelings and judgments. It fills to overflowing with light and pops, releasing these transformed energies back into your center. These are enlightened energies that are now free of their bonds. You may now choose to use this energy as you wish.

Continue this process with gradually more uncomfortable images. (You may need to repeat this process with some images more than once.)

Be aware of any further communication from your guides. Fully feel the transformation of this process. Be aware of a new sense of strength and wholeness.

Now become more aware of the sound of the drum calling you back to your center. Follow the rhythm up through your center and back to your physical body. Thank your guides for their continued guidance and protection and return to normal awareness.

Several years ago, I decided to clear out some of the last core shadow aspects that I had been consciously avoiding for most of my life. On one particular night, I entered a very dark door into the shadow world. In my journal, I wrote that as I entered, I "heard my own voice screaming and crying, talking, and complaining." I went down a bit more and the bottom fell out. I felt as though I was falling through an elevator shaft and I landed on a tiny island, smaller even than my own body.

I stood up on this little piece of damp land and waited to see what would happen. Versions of myself surrounded me. "Cold, pale young women, as though dead, crowded me." Three beings stood out from the rest. These comprised the core that had led to the hole in my center. They were the source of my anger, my perfectionism, and my low self-esteem. I accepted and integrated these aspects of my Self; these versions of myself at various points in life, frozen in time. Then I blew my feelings and judgments out into a bubble, just as I describe above in the Through the Shadow Meditation. Rather than it filling with light and popping, this bubble hardened, crystallized, and shattered like glass. A pure-white dove flew off from where the bubble had been, and, I wrote, "We smiled and felt happy as we watched it fly." I have not been the same since.

The journey through the shadow can be a difficult, even traumatic, experience. In truth, even just peering into the edges of the shadow can send many people running for cover. It is for this reason that we begin with the relatively simpler shadow aspects and work up to the deeply emotional ones. While I agree with the adage that all we have to fear is fear itself, in this situation it would be more accurate to say that all we have to fear are our own judgments about ourselves.

Since shadow aspects can be a challenge to uncover consciously, sometimes having an external focus can aid in recognizing them. Storytelling and the use of divination decks are highly effective methods for finessing these aspects into the light of our awareness.

Storytelling

Unfortunately, modern society has willingly lost so many of our stories that few of us remember how to create new ones. We rely on novels and movies for stories, but few of these have meanings that are applicable to our daily lives. In ancient times, shamans would create stories that were designed to externalize shadow aspects in individuals or strong emotions and conflicts among the community.

In this way, there was no finger-pointing and no embarrassment that might lead to further denial of issues that needed handling. Furthermore, it was understood that we often do not see ourselves and our actions as others do. Certainly not everyone is able to recognize themselves in the stories, but this provides a more comfortable first step to encouraging insight into how we are being perceived by the community.

Often through listening to a healer's story, the person in need is able to see his or her actions more objectively. This also offers the individual a view into the effects of these behaviors on other people and other things. A truly gifted storyteller can create characters of each individual issue and shadow aspect, allowing them to be more clearly seen. Depending on the worldview of each individual, the story characters may take human or animal form.

Using a hypothetical situation of a man who finds ignorance and prejudice everywhere, we can devise a very basic story based on the shadow aspects the healer finds through journeying or other divination methods. Let's assume that the healer found that, although this man had a healthy ego, he had underlying self-esteem issues and felt that he did not receive the recognition or respect he deserved in life. The healer also found that this man is highly critical of others and exhibits prejudicial behaviors himself.

This healer might devise a story of a bird that tried to build its nest in the highest tree so it could have privacy and isolation from other animals. The males of this particular species are very colorful and this one took an almost obsessive pride in its plumage, hiding during molting season and fearing to get dirty. He looked down on other animals so much that he refused to be seen with any of the females of his species because they lacked the beautiful colors.

Although this bird knew he was lonely, he didn't want to let any of the other birds see his loneliness, believing it to be a weakness they would not respect. He made a big deal out of saying that the mating rituals of other males were silly displays and the caretaking of the young and mates was degrading. As a result, this bird never mated. He grew to be an old, lonely bird with faded feathers and died alone, having never passed on his genes to a new generation.

These stories are often told seemingly as an afterthought. They are never obviously directed at the person in need and they are not told in an accusatory manner. Whether we are testing to see how intuitive a person is, or whether we feel this person is ready to begin to recognize some of these issues, we are careful about the context and manner in which the stories are told. It is important to keep in mind that this is a gentle externalization of shadow aspects.

Divination Decks

I know many healers who will use divination decks in their healing work. They may use them in preparation for a session to get an idea of what energies are present, or what aspects of Self may need balancing for the person in need. Some healers use decks as part of the healing session, and involve the person in need of healing in the process. They find that this involves the person from the very beginning, and it offers him or her a tangible experience on which to build.

The beauty of divination decks is that they have so many possibilities, if we merely apply imagination to the process. Most of us tend to choose decks that have themes or images that speak to us in some way. It is for this reason that such a huge variety is available today. There is something available that resonates for each of us.

The spreads outlined in the booklets that accompany each of these decks are very useful. These offer us clues to the energies present in a situation, and may indicate a possible way through difficulties. The suggested divinatory meanings provide basic possibilities, but they cannot include all potential meanings for the symbolism of the image. It is a good place to start, but to obtain the greatest benefit we must take this one step deeper.

Healers should be encouraged to take some time to sit with their deck. Peruse the meanings offered in the deck's booklet, but record any additional thoughts or feelings that may come up as you go through the cards. Not only does this personalize the deck, but it also increases the deck's effectiveness for you and anyone with whom you may work.

Deck Journeys

The simplest way for an experienced journeyer to benefit from divination decks is to explore each card visually in normal consciousness before entering the trance. Get a good mental image of the card and take that image into your journey. If you have a specific question or if this card showed up in a particular spot in a reading, take that into the journey along with the card image. Allow these intents and images to guide you as the journey develops on its own.

Another route to making your readings more shamanic is to combine a bit of storytelling with journeying. As you explore the card in this reality, create a story based on the image and its symbols. Use your imagination to develop a way to enter the card image and gain the information you need. This will serve as an outline for the shamanic journey.

For example, perhaps you are using the *Celtic Dragon Tarot* by D. J. Conway and Lisa Hunt. In your spread, the Hermit card turned up representing you. This card shows an old, green dragon sitting on a mountain ledge with a cave opening barely visible behind him. The dragon is poring over a book and there are other books and scrolls nearby. The roots of one of the small, twisted trees extend over the face of the cliff below him. Spirals and faces can be seen in the rocks surrounding him.

Your journey may begin with you approaching the dragon from the bottom of the cliff. You may call up to him and he may look up from his book long enough for you to ask a question. This may lead to a discussion or a journey with him in some way.

There are as many alternatives to this as there are readers of divination decks. I may prefer to climb up to him on the roots of the tree while someone else may find they approach him from within the cave. The dragon may never acknowledge your presence, and yet the images in the rocks may change or take you into a journey. Clear your mind and allow the outline to arise from your own inspiration.

Shadow aspects cannot hurt us unless we give them the power to do so. It is not in their best interests to harm us. They are like little children who have been so ignored that they need to act up in order to gain attention from their parents. They must reassert themselves to stay alive. In doing so, they keep us alive. These shadow aspects are our keys to wholeness and balance. They continue to affect our lives, attract people and situations to mirror us, and generally annoy us until we acknowledge them and end the cycle of fear and denial.

The shadow side is not something to be conquered or eliminated. It is an integral part of the human condition and simply needs to be acknowledged and explored. All of us—healers in particular—must be honest with others and ourselves in order to be *real*. This honesty and awareness of the shadow side is essential for accurate diagnoses and deciding the best course of action for anyone who comes to us for healing.

Perfect people with no issues, no history, and no *realness* have no frame of reference from which to understand suffering. This is why the Wounded Healer is so effective. These are people who have been there. We know about suffering. We have direct, often physical, reference points for pain, sorrow, anger, fear, and more. We also know about creating our own suffering and how it feels to hurt others, even unintentionally.

Healers do not strive to be perfect, nor should they project that type of persona. It is unfortunate that people may be made to feel that they must be beyond reproach with ideal lives and bodies in order to be acceptable as a teacher or healer. Those who are real are somehow seen as flawed and therefore not worthy. Many modern people seek an unreal image that will usually evade them. Even if they attain that perfect life and body, it often does not make them happy, and it certainly does not last forever.

Many modern people attempt to fill the hole left underneath this perfect persona with food, alcohol, material possessions, and superficial relationships. A healer's job is to help the person in need find a real way to fill that hole. This is done through restoring balance, by empowering the individual's true Self, by restoring one's connections to All That Is, and by re-establishing healthy contact with the shadow side.

9

RETRIEVAL AND EXTRACTION

Retrieval and extraction are the two most recognizable shamanic healing methods known to modern society. These techniques have been popularized by Sandra Ingerman's groundbreaking book *Soul Retrieval* (HarperCollins, 1991) and shamanic schools that train shamanic counselors in these methods. It is commendable that these individuals and groups have attempted to properly train people in retrieval and extraction.

However, there have been two unfortunate results of the newfound popularity of these techniques. The first is that many people do not fully understand what they are and how they can be expected to work. These people are often led to believe that these are "magic" cures, bringing health and happiness after only one or two sessions.

The second result is linked to the first one. There is now a plethora of soul retrieval counselors, practitioners, shamans, and so on. I like to call them the Soul Retrievers and many are quite good. Sadly, not all of these people have experience or training in these methods and may contribute to the perception of them as quick and easy, though expensive, cures.

This is why I have chosen to devote this chapter to retrieval and extraction. One cannot make an informed choice as to method or practitioner without an understanding of the process and the expected results. Shamanic healing is not covered by insurance. This is not a drug or medical procedure with a list of potential risks and a percentage probability of success.

I cannot emphasize the partnership aspect of shamanic healing enough. While a truly powerful shaman working on an individual with sufficient belief is likely to be extremely successful, that belief is part of the role of the person in need in this healing. In many cases, healing is a rather long process that is only possible through the active participation of the person in need and the willingness on the part of the healer to follow through.

The truth is that healing partnerships empower the person in need in ways that are not possible through mainstream medicine or anything that promises easy or immediate relief. The individual seeking healing must be willing to face difficult memories or aspects of Self, to be vulnerable and honest with oneself, and to take responsibility for one's experience of life. This may mean making difficult life choices, admitting wrongdoing, apologizing, or facing the mirror every day in honesty in order to build integrity.

For the healer, this is where the Partnership Brochure or information sheet (see chapter 2) comes into play. Holding these discussions early on and handing the person in need something to review on his or her own regarding this process empowers the relationship and protects both of you in the long run. All cards are on the table and the process can proceed in complete honesty—at least on the part of the healer—from that point on.

Soul Retrieval

Soul retrieval is a term that is commonly used to denote the return of lost fragments of the spirit. The shamanic perception of this is that the soul can shatter or parts can splinter off due to some sort of trauma. This trauma need not be something as intense as physical abuse or a life-threatening injury. Fragmentation can occur through the loss of a relationship or a departed loved one. It can happen as the result of a perceived failure, an embarrassment, or a frightening situation.

This concept has been incorporated into modern psychological thought in the theories regarding submerged subconscious impulses. The main difference is the shamanic perception that the soul or spirit has actually fragmented and may have become lost in the Otherworlds somewhere. It is also true that modern psychology generally holds that this splitting of the conscious awareness only occurs as the result of intense trauma. Shamanic practitioners recognize that trauma is relative and what causes the soul of one person to splinter may seem insignificant to another individual.

There is a significant difference between the perception of the psychologist and the shaman. The psychologist usually believes the subconscious, or shadow, to be a mysterious place beyond conscious awareness that is not truly real nor can it be mapped. To the shaman, these Otherworlds are very real and they contain specific landmarks and definite areas, just as our world does.

Recent advances in modern physics, specifically string theory, support this shamanic perspective. They suggest that our reality is simply a membrane floating within a higher-dimensional space. Other realities may only lie millimeters apart from our universe and some may be quite similar to ours.

For the shaman, knowledge of the location of the fragments and the properties of the specific world within which they reside are vital to the process of successfully returning them to the person in need. The shaman is qualified to go in search of these fragments due to a knowledge of and ability to further explore the Otherworlds. Shamans know the methods necessary to find soul fragments and have the capability of successfully retrieving them for those they are called to heal without placing anyone in danger in the process.

The retrieval or restoration of these fragments may result in the return of lost memories, power, and energy. As I wrote in the beginning of this chapter, soul retrieval is quite common these days. In many areas of the United States and Europe, at least one person can be found advertising their services in soul retrieval work. Even over the Internet, people offer to do this long distance or through your computer. It is often written up in short articles in various publications and made to sound like the quick fix for which modern society wishes.

Soul retrieval can be incredibly powerful. Many people have experienced life-changing healing and overwhelming empowerment through a single retrieval process, but there is another side to this. It is rarely a magic pill to the ideal life.

There are many people who have experienced a return to their former state of being after the glow of altered states has worn off. There are also too many people who have paid their money and had traumatic memories returned to them with no preparation or follow-up. These people experienced even more fragmentation and were left to deal with it on their own unless they were prepared to fork over another sixty bucks or whatever the going rate was at the time.

Certainly, the vast majority of shamanic practitioners are honest and honorable. They have received training and are fully dedicated to creating and supporting the healing of those who come to them. However, as a healer, you must be aware that unethical or misguided individuals are advertising their services and finding clients. It is quite possible that in the course of your practice you will come in contact with someone who has been burned by them.

A healer does not offer judgment regarding the talents or practices of another healer to the people that come in seeking healing. Most of the time we do not have sufficient knowledge to make such judgments and that would be an unethical tactic. When faced with people who have been hurt—whether the harm is real or perceived—we offer honesty regarding the process and our own methods. We let them know that we cannot guarantee a quick and glorious cure and we explain the healing partnership.

As a healer offering retrieval and extraction, you are likely to meet people who have read a book or two on shamanism and are certain of the process they need. They just need someone to do it for them. These people will come in insisting on retrieval when it is clear to you that what they really need is extraction. They may demand extraction when you feel a period of preliminary work needs to be done before getting into these more involved procedures.

Again, this is where we need to stress the concept of partnership in healing. While the healer is not the medical god that a mainstream doctor is often perceived as, we are also not servants to those who come to us for healing, even if there is to be a monetary exchange. This exchange is not simply buying services, like a blood test or antibiotics. The exchange is just that—an exchange of energy for the work we do on their behalf.

In these cases, you should explain that you will be communicating with spirit guides on this person's behalf. It is probable that you will also undertake a shamanic journey on your own time before making a decision on how to proceed. If your spirit guides tell you not to go ahead with soul retrieval, you are honor-bound to listen to that advice rather than simply giving the person what he or she requested.

If retrieval or extraction is required, inform the individual that he or she will need to have some personal support available. You are well within your rights to insist that someone drive this person to and from the session and stay with this person for a period of time at home. A support system is often vital to success. If you feel strongly about this or have received a message to this effect from spirit guidance, you will not move forward without the presence of some form of support for those that seek healing. You might first work toward helping the person in need find a support system of like-minded people.

Generally, the first plan of action is the power retrieval. This is often experienced as the return of a vital power animal. However, it may also manifest as the return of any important spirit guide or simply as a recovery of energy or attention. This is necessary to the process in that it provides the person in need with the essential power or energy to maintain the return and reintegration of any lost soul fragments. It provides a more solid and stable place for those soul parts to come home to. This not only makes it more likely that they will stay, but it also increases the ease with which they will return.

Many people, particularly those not familiar with a shamanic path, will experience this return as an increased ability to focus. We lose power along with various soul fragments. This is a self-preservation strategy and is extremely important in preserving the organism. However, each loss opens a hole in the energy field or fixes energy and attention on the fragment. Either way, we lose power.

In *Pagan Parenting,* I describe this using the analogy of a garden hose.[1] Each hole allows our energy (the water flowing through the hose) to escape, reducing the amount of power we have available to us (at the end of the hose) for conscious creation. The fixation of attention through soul fragmentation or energy blockage acts in a similar way by impairing the flow of energy and reducing the amount of free energy we have available to us for creation. Attention becomes scattered or a majority of it is stuck in one area. We are unable to focus and meditation can become virtually impossible.

This lack of energy or power often results in a lack of physical vitality. The individual may frequently feel tired or lack motivation to get up and move the body. A lack of flow through the body can create illness, obesity, and injury. Those areas of the body that contain these energy leaks may wither or develop chronic aches and pains.

---

1. Madden, *Pagan Parenting,* 59–60.

This may also manifest as a loss of will. People who have lost their power can become susceptible to cults or gangs. They may develop addictive personalities, becoming obsessed with alcohol, drugs, other people, or material things. There are other less extreme effects of this condition as well, such as continual failure, self-sabotage, or a handling of all situations through excessive joking or anger.

We may also lose power through a loss of spirit guides and guardians. There are various reasons why this may happen. These include a lack of attention, a refusal to acknowledge their influence, and a giving up of one's own power. I have to say that I have very rarely encountered an individual who had lost all spirit guides and guardians.

It is far more common for people to block the energy and communication that comes from spirit guides. Many times I have worked with individuals who had lost personal power. In most cases, a spirit guide or power animal was still with them, waiting for the opportunity to be of service. Once the blocks and fear were released, the spirit ally was able to re-enter the life of the chosen individual and begin the process of restoring power.

This is usually a lifelong or clan guardian that remains with the individual even when their very presence is denied and blocked. I do not intend to contradict those who have written that power animals may leave for various reasons. This does occur. In my experience, however, those allies that leave are more likely to be transient or situation-specific guides.

I grew up in the home of a deathwalker, so spirits were always present. Our house was also home to Nature spirits, departed loved ones, ancestral spirits, and other spirit guides. It was important to know who was just a recently departed family member (and no more advanced than we were), and who was a true spirit guide. How to tell the difference was never really explained to me; it was something that you came to recognize over time.

Those spirits that came for a specific reason or with a definite lesson always appeared to be more obvious than the others. They disturbed the normal resonance of the house by introducing a new type of energy. It was usually clear for which of us these beings were there. However, sometimes I was oblivious.

One night after doing some hypnotherapy work together, my mother went out to the front porch for a cigarette. She came back in very quickly to tell me that someone wanted to speak with me. She said "he" was not there for her and I didn't have much choice about it. So I went. He was there for a very specific healing that took most of the night and then he was gone.

In most indigenous cultures, it is understood that there is a clan guardian. Among Native American peoples this is often indicated as part of the name of those in the clan. My Saami ancestors believed that many of our animal allies were inherited from our parents. These allies could also be earned and "bought" or they would choose a Saami youth on their own. Specific conditions and tests were required of the youth before the ally would work with him or her.

We each have our allies from the Otherworlds. Whether you name them as power animals, animal allies, or spirit guides and guardians, they are there to teach, guide, and protect us. Some are with us throughout our lives, possibly unseen and unacknowledged. In some cases, these do appear to be clan or familial guardians. In other situations, they may be guides that have been with the individual soul for more than one incarnation, or they may be specific to this lifetime.

Whether we actually lose these guides or simply block them from interacting with our lives, the end result is the same. We do not benefit from their guidance and protection. The power that they brought to us is effectively gone. These guides affect our lives in more ways than we might imagine. They impact our relationships, our successes, our physical and emotional health, and more.

The power that our guides bring to us is what we restore during power retrieval, and this is essential to the process of reintegration. Without the ability to interact with a being of power—whether that is perceived to be external to us or not—we are not capable of maintaining restored soul fragments. The potential benefits of soul retrieval will be lost.

I should note that some people view power retrieval as a separate process from soul retrieval, while others believe them to be essentially the same. There are many people who see the loss of power or power animals to be a loss of soul parts. How you perceive this is irrelevant as long as it works for you. I separate the two here for purposes of clarity and ease.

Not everyone requires this power retrieval prior to soul retrieval. While it is very common, there are individuals who have retained or recovered enough power that this becomes unnecessary. The decision is always left to the spirit guides of the healer and the person in need. It is very important that we, as healers, do not get caught up in the ego. We must be able to release how much we know or how good we believe we are. Once we fall into that trap, our every judgment is suspect because it originates from within a very limited belief system that is dominated by the protection of the personality.

Below, I outline a basic power animal retrieval journey to be done within sacred space. This exercise can be done for oneself, mainly for minor or obvious fragments. I would not recommend that the healer offer this exercise to a person in need to perform alone unless you have a very strong feeling about it and are convinced of the individual's journeying ability and emotional stability.

When performing this exercise for oneself, promise to honor and work with the being or image you encounter. If it refuses, ask why. If it accepts, embrace it tightly and return to your physical body. Before opening your eyes in this world, clasp your hands in front of you and see this being return in your arms. Feel it merge with you before letting go and opening your eyes.

When performing this exercise for another person, it is preferable that it be done with that person present. You may both lie down on the floor near each other, or sit in chairs next to each other. The only requirement is that the person be close enough that you can simply reach out and touch him or her at the end of the journey.

POWER ANIMAL RETRIEVAL

Create a sacred space and enter the trance state with the intent to find a lost power animal that has relevance to the healing you are working on.

Allow yourself to be drawn to whatever world you feel pulls you. If you do not feel immediately drawn, head to the Lowerworld by your usual method. As you enter this world, ask that the lost power animal of the individual you are journeying for meet you.

Wander around wherever you like. Be aware of your surroundings, how you feel, and any beings that you meet along the way. Ask those that approach you if they are the lost power animals you seek.

You will know your power animals in one of two ways. You will see the same individual three times or one specific animal will come and teach you a special song that is to be taught to the person for whom you are journeying. Allow the experience to unfold as it will.

Ask this being to return with you and reintegrate with the person in need. Promise to teach this person how to honor it and work with it. If it refuses, ask why. If it accepts, embrace it tightly and return to your physical body.

Before opening your eyes in this world, clasp your hands in front of you. Feel the presence of this power animal in your arms. Lean over to the person you have journeyed for and place your hands on his or her shoulders. Feel the being between you and breathe this power animal into their energy field. See the two of them merge before letting go and opening your eyes.

The processes of power retrieval and soul retrieval are basically the same. The healer will enter the shamanic journey with a specific intent. He or she will then journey in search of the power animal or soul fragment that is missing. Often the healer is able to return and restore it without event. Sometimes special techniques and even trickery are necessary to convince the being or fragment to return.

In modern times, the free soul has been called a *light body* in a descriptive term referring to the energy state of this body. It is often seen as light that is beyond the normal range of human sight. Circumpolar cultures have described the shapeshifting travels of the shaman as rays of the sun or the aurora borealis. Central Asian shamans have been known to hook spirit fragments from rays emanated by healing deities through sending out this free-soul energy in rays. These rays go out into the Otherworlds in search of the fragments, hook them, and bring them back to the shaman. This is a technique that has worked well for me and I encourage you to experiment with it.

In many indigenous cultures, it was understood that the free soul, which is the part of us that journeys out of body, could wander into places it should not be and become stuck or lost. It was equally possible for the soul to be detained in the Lands of the Dead by ancestors or departed loved ones, or to be stolen for various reasons. These were the situations when a shaman was called upon for the most vital type of healing.

In these cases, the shaman would offer gifts or sacrifices to the beings that held the soul or soul fragment. I know very few modern healers who hold to this custom, but many traditional shamans still perform these healings in the same way. What method you choose will depend on your beliefs.

The shaman was recognized as one with an extraordinary ability to travel out of body. This individual was known to have traveled into the Lands of the Dead and returned as a stronger, more capable being. This was the one person in the community who had intimate knowledge of the roads of the Otherworlds. Therefore, the shaman was the only one with the ability to restore lost or stolen souls.

This is not the case today, for a variety of reasons. Many people who might not meet the criteria for being a Shaman or a traditional shaman have the training and experience to perform successful soul retrievals. Various shamanism schools have, as one of their goals, the intent to fully train people in shamanic counseling and soul retrieval. These people have undergone a considerable amount of focused training under the supervision of an experienced shamanic practitioner.

Many experienced healers and shamans reject the idea of a Shaman School, and in all honesty, these "certified" healers do not necessarily have a great deal of experience on their own.[2] However, the certificate is an easy way for you to prove you have had the training you claim. It can put those that come to you at some degree of ease, knowing that you have tangible evidence of your training.

Some people prefer to heal themselves as much as possible without relying on others. Healers tend to take a fair amount of their own healing on themselves. There are obvious pros and cons to this approach. Certainly, it is more convenient and less expensive. You stand to learn a great deal through the process and not all of us have access to another shamanic healer.

However, healing oneself can also be an escape or avoidance technique. We may be subject to our own blocks and resistance, thereby missing or avoiding work that really needs to be done. This is particularly true early on in your path, before you have really come to know your Self and have learned to listen to spirit guidance. For the healer, it can be a case of ego interference and not wanting to be vulnerable to other healers. In any case, the reasons for avoiding work with other healers should be explored.

Many people do not believe that we can retrieve parts of our own souls. While they admit that some soul fragments may return spontaneously, their experience has shown them that it usually requires an experienced healer to intervene on the behalf of the person in need.

---

2. Reputable schools, such as Ardantane's School of Shamanic Studies and the Foundation for Shamanic Studies, require extensive training.

In general and particularly regarding significant or long-term fragmentation, I would agree with this.

However, fragments do spontaneously return under certain conditions and an experienced practitioner is perfectly capable of retrieving even traumatic fragments on his or her own. Developing this ability, particularly to clear the small bits of fragmentation that occur through living in this world, is something every healer should be encouraged to develop. This is part of the continual process of growth and training that we should not allow ourselves to halt once we become Healers.

When an individual has done a great deal of personal work to clear shadow aspects and regain confidence and personal power, the conditions necessary for soul fragments to return on their own are created. These are generally not the deepest and most painful fragments, but with each one that returns, we regain even more power and stability, thereby allowing more difficult fragments to come forth for reintegration.

This is often experienced as a noticeable increase in self-confidence and self-esteem, along with a less pronounced need for external validation. It is often a subtle and gradual process. Suddenly one day, we realize that we feel stronger and more complete than we did a few years ago. It is a wonderfully freeing feeling.

When I was a freshman in college, after having left high school after three years because I was so motivated to do advanced academic work, I was gang-raped and knifed on campus. This took place near the end of my first semester at school. It was utterly devastating to me. I had been a naïve and trusting teen who believed if I treated others well, then I would be treated in the same way.

Since I had been trained since childhood to be able to retrieve details and images no matter what circumstances surrounded them, I had complete and total memory of the event. This was something the police were not equipped to believe, since they had seen most rape victims block all memories. While I was able to give descriptions and details to the police, I was not able to escape the memories at a time when that was exactly what I needed.

I lost significant soul fragments but retained the images. Every time I needed to repeat the story, more fragmentation occurred. I disappeared into destructive behaviors and my personality noticeably changed, as did my performance in school. I had all the classical symptoms of avoidance and repression, yet I refused to give in and "let them beat me again."

This created several painful holes in me that remained an integral part of my being for many years. On several occasions, I worked with healers who attempted to help me release the trauma and reintegrate those fragments. Nothing worked because I was not ready.

Finally, many years later after having done extensive work on my "easier" shadow aspects, I reached a point of clarity and personal power. I had established deep and open communication with spirit guides and did not fight every suggestion they made. It was only then that I was able to return to that experience and move through it to healing. This was something I needed to do on my own and it was quite effective.

So it is possible to be able to retrieve your own fragments, but it is not easy. It may take decades of intense shamanic work to reach that point. This may be something you choose to experiment with for relatively simpler fragments. However, I would caution you not to get so caught up in early success and ego-stroking that you delude yourself into believing you are healing what you are not. It is a strong and intelligent healer who knows when to ask others for help.

Shamanically, we perceive soul fragments to exist somewhere in the personal shadow side, which may lie in the Otherworlds. It may be seen as a fixed event in time. These fragments are frequently observed within the physical and energy bodies by shamanic and psychic healers.

Just as the free and body souls integrate into the physical body to create life and consciousness, so do we store past fragments and memories here. Great success has been had in releasing these fragments through various yogic techniques and deep tissue bodywork. A gentler method is available for use by the individual without need of another person.

The following exercise is based on one method of releasing past fragments a former yoga teacher taught my mother and me many years ago. I have seen variations on the basic concept in other places since then, but the method outlined here has proven to be of tremendous benefit for my family. I highly recommend that you record this and play it back as a guided meditation. You should also feel free to add any points for experimentation or where you have had physical issues.

As a taped meditation, you may use it whenever you wish. This prevents the necessity of splitting your focus in order to remember what point to go to next. It also provides a reminder to keep moving and to return at the end of the tape.

It is quite likely that you will experience a variety of effects with this process. You may find that you have occasionally moved on to a point with no memory of the previous points. You may experience mental, emotional, or physical discomfort.

If you are able, try to move through this. If it becomes more than simple discomfort, discontinue the process and give it another try later on. If you are unable to get through it without extreme discomfort, consult a professional healer.

You may fall asleep during this meditation. If this happens, that is perfectly fine. You will continue to experience the meditation without the involvement of your conscious mind and you will achieve some benefit that may lead to a more conscious process in the future. If you miss the count up at the end, you will simply fall into normal sleep and awaken as usual.

Every member of my family has experienced one, if not all, of these possibilities of discomfort or sleep when working with this technique. For months, my mother would blank out at one particular point and return to conscious awareness at the same other point. My husband and father have a tendency to fall asleep during it. I have experienced my mind wandering and the same type of blank spots as my mother at various spots depending on what was going on in my life.

Don't feel inadequate if these things happen to you. Just because you are a healer does not mean you don't retain lingering fragments of your own. If they happen to the people you are led to use this technique with, be sure to encourage them to stick with it. Let them know that these experiences are not uncommon. They are simply an indication that we are beginning to handle stored fragments.

This exercise is to be done in a safe space where you will not be disturbed for at least one hour. As you direct your attention to various points on your body, breathe deeply into each point. Accept whatever comes up without judgment and just allow it to pass through. Allow each pause to last for a few seconds.

FREEING FRAGMENTS IN THE PHYSICAL BODY

Breathing deeply, count yourself down from ten to one. Take your time and periodically stop to remind yourself to breathe deeply. Say to yourself that you are moving into a deeper, relaxed, and safe state of mind.

Repeat the countdown once.

Place your full attention on the center of your forehead. [*pause*] Move your attention to the base of your head at the nape of your neck. [*pause*] Move your attention back to the center of your forehead. [*pause*]

Move your attention to the hollow of your neck. [*pause*] Move your attention to your left shoulder. [*pause*] Move your attention to your left elbow. [*pause*] Move your attention to your left wrist. [*pause*] Move your attention to the center of your left palm. [*pause*] Retracing these points, return your attention to the hollow of your neck.

Move your attention to your right shoulder. [*pause*] Move your attention to your right elbow. [*pause*] Move your attention to your right wrist. [*pause*] Move your attention to the center of your right palm. [*pause*] Retracing these points, return your attention to the hollow of your neck.

Move your attention to the center of your chest. [*pause*] Move your attention to your left nipple. [*pause*] Move your attention to your right nipple. [*pause*] Move your attention to your solar plexus. [*pause*] Move your attention to the center of your abdomen. [*pause*] Move your attention to your genitals. [*pause*]

Move your attention to your left hip. [*pause*] Move your attention to your left knee. [*pause*] Move your attention to your left ankle. [*pause*] Move your attention to the bottom of your left foot. [*pause*] Retracing these points, move your attention to the center of your abdomen.

Move your attention to your right hip. [*pause*] Move your attention to your right knee. [*pause*] Move your attention to your right ankle. [*pause*] Move your attention to the bottom of your right foot. [*pause*] Retracing these points, move your attention to the center of your abdomen.

Move your attention to your left buttock. [*pause*] Move your attention to your right buttock. [*pause*] Move your attention to the small of your back. [*pause*] Move your attention to the center of your back. [*pause*] Move your attention to the space between your shoulder blades. [*pause*] Move your attention to your left shoulder blade. [*pause*] Move your attention to your right shoulder blade. [*pause*] Move your attention to the base of your neck. [*pause*] Move your attention to the top of your head. [*pause*] Move your attention to the center of your forehead.

Count yourself back up from one to ten. Take your time and periodically remind yourself that you are coming up slowly and that, at the count of one, you will be wide awake, feeling full of energy, and perfectly safe.

The process of soul retrieval can be a particularly powerful healing method. Some people use it weekly while others use it only as a last resort. The truth is that, like all healing, it is a lifelong process. It may take a lifetime to fully recover fragments from a truly horrific experience. On the other hand, even those individuals who do not experience anything deeply traumatic may experience smaller fragmentations as they go about their everyday lives.

The key to rising above this continual fragmentation is to work to retain your personal power and your connections to spirit guides and All That Is. This is vital to anyone involved in healing work. Resist the urge to block the flow of energy and to avoid challenging experiences. It may seem fine to do so on occasion, but once you get into the habit, it becomes automatic. It is far more preferable to handle the experience at hand than have to go back years later and deal with a bigger mass of shadows and fragments that has resulted from denial and resistance.

Extraction

The process of healing through shamanic extraction is possibly one of the most intriguing of the shamanic healing processes. It is based on the belief that a foreign energy has become embedded in the individual's energy field and is causing illness or other problems. This is not necessarily something "bad," although it may be. It is simply something that is not a normal part of the individual's energy field and does not belong there.

Most healers will perceive these foreign objects—often called intrusions—as something personally repulsive. Traditional images include insects, scorpions, and other arachnids, snakes and worms, fanged animals, or dull and dark masses. I have also seen them as knives and shards of glass or ice. This symbolism frequently reflects the fact that the intrusion is causing damage and occasionally indicates the source of the intrusion.

Shamanic healers who are also possessed of psychic Sight can often see these intrusions simply by looking at a person, although some need to enter a light trance first. There are healers who use a ritually consecrated mirror to see the intrusions in the reflection. Some healers will find intrusions by using the pendulum or feeling in the person's energy field with their hands. Most shamanic healers, however, use the journey for diagnosing intrusions or possession.

Using the journey to diagnose intrusions is made even more effective if the person seeking healing has developed an ability to use the shamanic journey. For healing purposes, the healer can undertake a journey similar to the retrieval journey in which healer and individual journey together. The healer may go out of body and assist the free soul of the person in need, or healer and individual may choose to meet at a prearranged Otherworld location. In this way, the healer is able to clearly see any blocks or intrusions in the spirit.

The healer may be guided to initiate healing during this journey, and this can be quite effective. However, most healers will perform a separate extraction procedure when intrusions are found. Traditionally, this removal is done by either scooping out the intrusion using the hands or by sucking it out with the mouth.

Most modern healers prefer to work with the scooping method, believing it to be safer for the healer. The intrusion is considered more likely to become lodged in the body of the healer through the mouth method. Traditional healers take specific precautions to prevent this. Some hold special objects in their mouths while performing the extraction. Others will suck through a cloth or special band that catches the intrusions before they can enter the healer.

I do not recommend that anyone attempt to perform extraction without adequate preparation and development of shamanic abilities. Not only do you want to be as effective as possible in your healing sessions, but you also do not want to make yourself sick in the process. I also suggest that you work with a shamanic partner until you gain experience. This should be someone who can take over for you, bring you out of the journey, and perform healing on you if necessary. As always, healers should enlist the aid of their spirit guides before performing any of the methods described here.

The sucking method is much like the method of sucking out venom from a snake bite in that you suck very hard to draw out the entire intrusion. However, during the procedure, the healer does not touch the physical body of the person for whom the session is being held. It may require extensive sucking to remove every bit of intrusion and this is very important. Unless you remove all of it, it will grow back and may spread to other areas, just like a cancerous tumor.

The intrusion must be disposed of once it is completely removed. The method of disposal will depend on your training and your spirit guidance. I generally use water or fire to release and transform the energy. In some cultures, the healer uncovers the source of the intrusion and returns it to its original home. This is particularly true when the intrusion is believed to be that of a Nature spirit or local energy.

For the following ceremony, you should have a jar of water ready to transfer the intrusions into once you have removed them from the person in need. If you have decided to use the sucking technique, you should also have your cloth or preventive objects ready in the sacred space. Once the intrusion has been removed, place these objects in the jar of water for holding until disposal.

CEREMONY OF EXTRACTION

Create a sacred space in your preferred manner. Purify yourself and the individual for whom this ceremony is held.

Sing your power song.

Call upon your personal spirit guides and those of the person in need. Ask for their guidance and blessings in this work. Let them know you are open to their communication.

Have the person who is the healing focus lie down in the center of the space. Sitting by this person's side, allow your trance to deepen. Using your hands, feel the intrusion. Get a sense of its mass, its depth, and its temperature.

Begin to scoop or pull out the intrusion, placing it in the jar of water as you get pieces of it out. Continue this process until you cannot find any intrusion left.

Take a deep breath and allow your trance to deepen. Sing your power song once more and allow it to become a healing song if you feel drawn to do so. Look at the person in need with your shamanic sight to see if anything remains of this intrusion. Scan the body for additional intrusions. You may prefer to feel the energy field or use the pendulum for this. If you find anything else, repeat the scooping and pulling process.

Once the person is clear of intrusions, channel clear, healing energy into his or her field, paying particular attention to where the intrusions were removed. See this person full of light energy.

Ask the person to sit up and return to normal consciousness. You may wish to hold any discussions now within the sacred space. Allow time for any messages to come through or for any emotional release that may occur.

Thank all those who joined in this ceremony for their guidance and blessings. Invite the person in need to thank his or her own spirit guides as well as any others to whom he or she may wish to express gratitude.

Close the sacred space in your preferred manner and dispose of the intrusion with respect.

It is dangerous to treat intrusions with disrespect or to react childishly to the fact that this energy has caused harm. These are rarely energies that intended to cause illness or injury. To act in an honorable manner and treat all things with respect maintains the flow of power. It also protects against the types of illnesses that result from a lack of integrity and bad behavior.

People who offer no respect to the spirits run the risk of angering them. At the very least, they are not likely to gain their blessings. By respect, I do not mean that we treat them like gods. We simply treat them as we would like to be treated. When we are treated poorly, we are not motivated to assist and protect those who abuse us. When we are treated well, we may go out of our way to help others.

It is for this reason that we dispose of intrusions with respect. We refrain from offering them any additional energy, such as may arise from fear or anger. We also give them no reason to return to the person in need or to follow the healer home.

Depossession

The process of depossession is, in effect, the extraction of an intruding spirit from the energy field of a person seeking healing. Shamanic healers recognize that people can pick up unwanted "guests" through out-of-body travel or being in a weakened state, such as occurs during illness, anesthesia, or soul loss. These beings may be lost spirits of the departed or those that deny they are dead. Due to a lack of death-walkers in modern times, these beings may have difficulty moving on to the next world and remain stuck here.

Some people have a natural tendency toward possession, also known as *channeling, mediumship,* and *being ridden* (in the Voudou tradition). This is something very different from how most of us receive messages from spirit guides. I have only allowed a spirit to share my body once and this was for a short-term special purpose. It was not entirely unpleasant, but I knew the spirit and was quite confident she was not planning to stay.

On the other hand, my mother has a great ability in this area. It is not an ability that she enjoys much of the time. When I was seven or eight years old, the father of a friend of hers died. He was unable to contact his son or anyone in the family so he came to her. He was desperate to communicate with his son and found his way to the closest person who could help him. He came in through a window one night and aggressively entered my mother's physical body. The voice that spoke from her mouth was most definitely not hers. He passed on his message and left as abruptly as he came. The situation with the man's son was resolved and we had no more visits from him.

These beings rarely intend to cause harm. They are usually looking to return to the living or are seeking attention and help. In the case of depossession, we now have two beings in need of care. Before proceeding, we need to heal the disembodied spirit first. Even if this is simply a being that normally resides in other realms, healers are responsible for ensuring that they do no harm. That means checking to see if the possessing spirit is in need of healing or assistance.

The process of healing a possessing spirit may require nothing more than a discussion with the spirit and a request to leave the body of the person in need. This will be especially easy if the spirit is a departed loved one who still cares for this person. Sometimes the situation calls for considerable persuasion or trickery. Force is used only as a last resort.

The extraction procedure outlined above is quite effective for removing those spirits who just do not want to leave. Rather than sucking or scooping, it is preferable to gently lift or pull the intruding spirit from the energy of the person in need. This may be experienced as helping it to stand and walk into the next world, or it may appear to be something like lifting out a baby. On occasion, it may take the form of shamanic symbols and may be very similar to the usual extraction of intrusions.

If significant force is required, any healer who does not have experience in these matters and does not have a fully qualified shamanic partner as back-up should contact a more experienced shaman and transfer the case to that individual.

Purification

Special purification ceremonies may be used for instances of intrusion or possession. These will vary depending on the amount of pressure or force needed to persuade the intruding energy to leave. Sometimes a purification ceremony may require actions that are intended to frighten the spirit out of the energy field of the person seeking healing.

As with the usual extraction and depossession procedures, this type of purification demands that the healer be trained and experienced. Shamanic strength and the ability to fight when necessary are requirements for a successful purification. It should be noted that some energies do not want to leave.

The following ceremony is a good outline of the process. The cord or cloth is to be tied around the person in need approximately six inches away from the location of the intrusion. The energy of the intrusion will be driven into this object, which will then be discarded. This person should be sitting or lying down and his or her arms and legs should not be crossed.

If the intrusion was sent by another individual, or if it was in any way caused by something that may be repeated, we need to include a method of protection at the end of the ceremony. This may be a special rock or some type of amulet. For small children, you may choose to make this in a way that will occupy the child's attention during the ceremony. You may attach small bells or something similar to it. This will also improve the chances that the child will continue to focus on this object once the ceremony is over, thus increasing the protective ability of the amulet.

I do not recommend that anyone attempt this alone unless you have considerable training and experience in handling serious situations. It is preferable to have at least two shamanic assistants present. I also suggest that the person seeking healing be the only person present without shamanic training. It is not unknown for intrusions to move out of one's body and attempt to find another host body for safety.

The initial ritual is to be done prior to the ceremony of purification. In this ritual, you will prepare a special cloth or cord to catch and hold the intrusion. You will also charge and bless a protective rock or amulet for the person in need.

PURIFICATION PREPARATION

Have the following items ready in your circle:
- The special cloth or cord
- A clean bag to hold this cloth or cord
- The rock or amulet

Create a sacred space in your preferred manner. Smudge or drum to completely clear yourself and your ritual area.

Sing your power song.

Call upon your personal spirit guides and those of the person seeking healing. Ask for their guidance and blessings in this work.

Place the special cloth or cord in the center of your circle. Create a smaller and more intensive sacred space around this item. Smudge or drum to completely clear it of all energies, including your own. Ask the Creator to clear this item and allow it to be used for the highest good of all concerned.

Place this cleared item in the clean bag. Touch it as little as possible as you place it in the bag.

Smudge or drum your energy field once again to completely clear yourself.

Take up the rock or amulet and offer it to the spirits of the directions. Smudge or drum to completely rid it of all energies, including your own. Ask that the spirit guides of the person in need and the Creator bless and heal the keeper of this item.

Sing a healing song or chant a specific incantation to charge this item with the healing that the person seeking healing requires. Ask that it function as a clear channel for healing energy and protection. You may also want to ask that it serve as a Medicine bag, holding personal power for this person and allowing free communication from spirit guides.

Continue this charging until you feel the item strongly resonate with the energy you intend.

Offer thanks to all those beings that joined you and blessed your work. Thank them for their continuing presence in your life and close the sacred space in your preferred manner.

CEREMONY OF PURIFICATION

Place your altar in the north of your circle. Have the following items ready on the altar:
- A prepared cord or piece of cloth
- A jar of water
- A source of purifying smoke
- A feather or fan
- A candle or oil lamp
- A ritual knife or sword

Create a sacred space in your preferred manner. Invoke the spirits of the directions and the Great Spirit or Creator and ask for guidance and blessings. Be sure to call upon your healing guides and the spirit guides of the person in need.

Smudge your energy field three times with the purifying smoke. Smudge the ritual space and then the energy of this person three times.

Sing your power song and allow it to develop into a healing song.

Using your hands, feel the intrusion. Get a sense of its mass, its depth, and its temperature. Wrap the cloth or cord around the person approximately six inches away from the boundary of the intrusion.

Take a deep breath and allow your trance to deepen. Sing a healing song or chant an incantation calling the intrusion toward the cloth or cord. Sing or chant until the intrusion has fully entered the cloth or cord.

Remove the cloth or cord and plunge it into the water, sealing the jar immediately with its top.

If the intrusion does not easily move into the cloth or cord, or if it refuses to stay there, you will need to use your ritual knife. You may prefer to cut the intrusion out of the energy field of the person seeking healing. Some traditional healers will charge the person and stab the air in front of the intrusion to frighten it away. Other healers will use the strength of the knife to spur their own fighting instinct and drive out the intrusion. You need to find what works best for you. Whatever your choice, be absolutely certain that you do not risk injury to anyone through the use of the knife.

Once the individual is clear of the intrusion, channel clear, healing energy into his or her field, paying particular attention to where the intrusion was removed. See the person full of this light energy.

Ask the person to sit up and return to normal consciousness. You may wish to hold any discussions now within the sacred space. Allow time for any messages to come through or for any emotional release that may occur.

Thank all those who joined in this ceremony for their guidance and blessings. Invite the person in need to thank his or her own spirit guides as well as any others to whom he or she may wish to express gratitude.

Close the sacred space in your preferred manner and dispose of the intrusion with respect.

These methods are advanced shamanic methods. Even skilled shamans frequently work with an assistant. It is traditional to perform these methods with the support of other shamans to hold protective energy and with shamanic drummers to drum away loose intrusions or prevent other disembodied spirits from coming in at a critical point.

It would be unethical and potentially dangerous for the beginning healer to attempt to use these methods before gaining a good amount of shamanic experience and training in healing methods. I offer them so that when you reach that point, you do not need to search for traditional methods or devise your own from scratch. In order to become the best healer you can, it is wise to start slowly and allow your abilities to develop in their own time. In this way, you increase your potential for great work and you honor all your relations in the process.

10

THE HEALING UNIVERSE

Shamanism is a Nature-centered spiritual path. Like many of the other Nature spiritualities, we find divinity in Nature. To us, the earth and heavens are living entities upon and within which reside an innumerable amount of other living beings that are perceived to be our teachers and relations. Each of us is an integral part of this interconnected cosmos and it is through Nature that our power flows.

This is obvious in the construction of our rituals, the general perceptions of the Otherworlds, and in our relationship to plants, stones, and animals as Teachers. We honor the Earth Mother and the Sky Father, although these genders and names may vary. Many of us feel we simply cannot breathe in the modern world without a Nature fix.

This need for the natural world is not limited to those on the shamanic path. Some of us are more aware of it than others, but everyone suffers when disconnected from Mother Earth. These wounds are evident in how we treat ourselves, each other, and the world in which we live. They manifest through all aspects of our lives, including health-care practices.

Studies of office workers have shown that those whose desks face windows with views of the natural world are less stressed and have fewer sick days than those with no windows or whose windows offer views of other buildings, parking lots, and so on. Other studies have shown that patients need fewer painkillers and recover from illnesses faster when they can see trees and other natural scenes from their windows.

The healing benefits and our innate need for some interaction with the natural world is obvious. Even those of us who feel no spiritual bond to Nature flock to parks and beaches to spend leisure time. This is something of which all of us—healers in particular—need to be aware.

As healers, we need to maintain an awareness of the possibilities that those coming to us for healing are feeling the effects of this disconnection from the natural world. We also should consider the potential benefit of deepening that connection for all those in need. It is my hope that you will choose to explore the connection between health and isolation from Nature further.

The Gaian Connection

Ecopsychologists and deep ecologists believe that most of our societal ills stem from our alienation from Nature. Similarly, the state of our planet depends largely on the mental and emotional health of humans. To these relatively new philosophies, our interactions with the natural world—good or bad—reflect our inner selves. They are, in a way, projections of our unconscious impulses and beliefs, just as our interactions with other people are often the result of projected issues.

I would add that both the health of our communities and the natural world also depend on our spiritual well-being. These fields are complex and fascinating studies in human history and psychology that should prove interesting to anyone involved with shamanism. In fact, several ecopsychologists believe that ecopsychology has its roots in shamanism.

As we are removed from natural cycles, we may lose that feeling of interconnection. We no longer perceive the earth, plants, and animals to be related to us. We are separate and frequently seen as superior to natural cycles and the dirty, primitive world of Nature. Nature becomes something to conquer, control, or eliminate. Our actions betray this lack of connection as we exhibit psychological conditions, physical illnesses, and destroy the land.

The cycle continues when we begin to experience our disconnected societies. We learn to disrespect each other and ourselves. We come to fear the natural world and create conditions to further distance ourselves. Our cultures become increasingly materialistic and unnatural. This results in poor treatment of the elderly and unhealthy images of the perfect life, of ridiculous wealth, and impossible physical goals that often require surgery to attain.

I am not implying that money, good looks, and nice stuff are inherently bad for us. However, an attachment to these things to the point where our self-image and confidence relies on their attainment is certainly unhealthy. Particularly in the Westernized world, consumerism has become an addiction. Luxury is wonderful but it can lead to dependence and a fear of the wildness of Nature.

It is sad to note that there are people who have only experienced ritual, meditation, or shamanic journeying indoors. I know pagans who have never communicated with a tree, a river, or an animal, except in their own meditations and journeys. We do not all need to go tramping miles out into the wilderness, however, if all our Nature spirituality is experienced beneath a man-made roof, we run the risk of it becoming a mental image rather than a deep communion.

Urban shamanism is a valuable aspect to the path and one that deserves more attention. However, we each need to find a way to develop a personal and direct relationship with Nature. Even if you merely sit in a city park and commune with the trees and animals, you are opening to the healing that the Earth will provide. This is something that shamanic healers should consider encouraging in all those that come to them for healing, even if their complaints are not related to a disconnection from the natural world.

My mother often says that Nature is her religion. Nothing else makes as much sense as the natural world, and all that we need flows through us in that connection. My great-aunt taught me that our strength and wisdom comes to us from above the stars, beneath the stones, and from all things in between. My grandfather ensured his daily connection to the Earth and Her creatures by becoming a park ranger. He instilled this combination of reverence and Family with the Earth in each of us.

When I was locked away in a laboratory for very long days, I craved wilderness. My husband and I spent most of our vacations and weekends that I did not have to work backpacking. My goal was to get at least ten miles away from any hint of human civilization, but these times were hard to come by and I needed to find a way to survive in the cavelike laboratories.

I made sure that my office and the labs had plenty of plants, and I would "veg out" for a minute or two, communing with these plants. I took at least one break each day for at least five minutes when I could just get outside and tune in to the sky, the earth, and any trees that were present.

In these ways, I made sure that I was not completely isolated from the natural world. Yet for me, it was much more than maintaining a feeling for my connections to All That Is; it was healing. I could feel the changes in my energy, my body, and my attitude from a high-stress job. Like many people, I suffered from stress-related illness and injury on occasion. When I kept to this communion, my physical and mental health was noticeably improved. Furthermore, I felt myself slipping into the modern mind-set of money, prestige, and single-minded focus. I didn't like who I could become if I let those connections slip away.

Most of us have felt the potential for healing inherent in the natural world. We have marveled at the glory of a sunset, taken deep breaths of the sea air, and stared up at the stars glittering in the night sky. This is poetry incarnate and it touches us at a very deep, often physical, level, but Nature can do much more than just make us feel a little less stressful after a hard day.

Some child psychologists have found that Nature often plays a role in maintaining the sanity of abused children. Children may see the natural world as an escape, a place where they can be free. Some children develop such a personal relationship with Nature that they feel the Earth Mother actually protects and comforts them. Abused children who have no access to the solace of the natural world may never heal from the psychological wounds inflicted during childhood abuse.

Nature has tremendous potential to bring healing. Sadly, many people refuse to open to this out of a fear of wildness or simply because they have lost the ability to recognize this wellspring of comfort and healing. Not only is the natural world filled with the manifestations of our spirit guides, it is replete with medicines and foodstuffs. Its very existence creates an energy that resonates with the healing rhythms of Mother Earth and Father Sky.

If we can tap into that energy, we, too, begin to resonate with healing. We find that we are never truly alone and that we will receive unconditional support in our work as healers. The natural world will ground sorrow and release pain. In its place, both healers and those in need are filled with joy and oneness. We can recall our real Selves in the wilderness and be who and what we truly feel. The trees don't care if we have a big house or a high-powered job.

This is the Source that needs remembering by healers and those seeking healing. Healers find that they are renewed and revitalized through Nature. We do those in need a great service if we can assist them in reconnecting to All Our Relations in a personal way. The exercise below is one way to begin doing that. It is simple and subtle. As such, it can be done in a city park or on a neighborhood street without causing any odd looks or comments.

CENTERING THROUGH THE SENSES

Sit or stand quietly in a place in Nature where you feel safe and are unlikely to be disturbed. Take a deep breath and breathe out all your tensions and all your worries. Ask the

Spirits of Place for their permission before moving forward with the exercise. If you feel strongly that permission is not given, try another place or another time.

Focus on your sight. Allow your eyes to relax. Rather than focusing on what you see, simply be with the process of seeing. Permit any thoughts that come up to pass through your mind and float away. Try not to categorize or label what you see. Enter into communion with the essence of the world around you. Become aware of any changes in your sight as your body slows and centers. You may notice light and shadow more, or you may be increasingly aware of new colors around you.

Now close your eyes and focus on your hearing. Don't strain to hear anything, just gently be with whatever you hear. Permit any thoughts that come up to pass through your mind and float away. Try not to categorize or label what you hear. Enter into communion with the essence of the world around you. Become aware of any changes in your hearing as your body slows and centers. Feel yourself grounding and opening to the natural world.

Change your focus to your sense of smell. Don't actively sniff the air, just gently observe whatever you smell. Permit any thoughts that come up to pass through your mind and float away. Try not to categorize or label what you smell. Enter into communion with the essence of the world around you. Become aware of any changes in your sense of smell as your body slows and centers. Feel yourself grounding and opening to the natural world.

Now focus on your sense of touch. Feel the earth beneath you, the sun and wind on your skin, your clothes, and the feel of your body. Permit any thoughts that come up to pass through your mind and float away. Try not to categorize or label what you feel. Enter into communion with the essence of the world around you. Become aware of any changes in how you feel as your body slows and centers. Feel yourself grounding and opening to the natural world.

Allow each of these senses to combine. Feel your entire body resonate with awareness. Permit any thoughts that come up to pass through your mind and float away. Try not to categorize or label what you feel. Enter into communion with All That Is. Become aware of any changes in how you feel as your body slows and centers. Feel yourself grounding and opening as you become one with the natural world.

After practicing with this exercise, those that come to you for healing may begin to feel a subtle difference in how they define themselves. Encourage them to be aware of where their boundaries are. Do they define themselves as their bodies or do they include beliefs and something rather indefinite called the mind? Perhaps they include their families, ancestors, or ethnic communities in the definition of Self. Guide them to consider how the natural world plays into this personal definition.

You should encourage those that come to you for healing to keep a journal or notebook of their own to record their experiences of the exercises you teach them. Discussing these experiences should become part of healing sessions. Not only will these journal entries let you know that the person is really doing the work you ask them to do, but they should also give you an idea of how the work is progressing and on what you need to focus.

Many of us—from ecopsychologists to native elders—deeply believe that the problems in our societies and the destructive changes to the natural world are subtly interwoven. This is really only subtle from a disconnected point of view. To those of us that maintain and honor both the natural world and each other, it is truly obvious.

Environmental medicine has only recently determined that one's environment may be hazardous to physical health, and even much of this is still debated. We now have terms for chemical sensitivity and "sick house syndrome." Yet the idea of environment—with the exception of abusive families—is not accepted as a potential cause for mental and emotional illness.

It is easy for us to recognize ourselves as victims—in fact, this is almost a way of life for many people—but to admit that we are the ones inflicting harm is a far more difficult task. Even more, to allow for the possibility that our own ills may be due to our personal and collective disrespect seems ridiculous to most modern people. Consider whether or not it is possible that we are reaping what we have sown in the world.

Most metaphysical people agree that we receive the type of energy we send out. If people are coming to you for shamanic healing, chances are good that they have a basic understanding of this concept. If this concept is true, then it is not really so far-fetched to think that the human race is now experiencing the manifest return of the destruction and dishonor we have poured onto our planet.

It may help to view this from a purely biological perspective. In any ecosystem, the top predator is often affected by the poison ingested by its prey and even that contained in its prey's prey. A process known as *bioaccumulation* occurs, concentrating these poisons with each step up the food web. It is common for wild animals to die of conditions such as heavy metal poisoning without ever having directly ingested the metals themselves. Their prey ingested it or ingested an animal that ingested it and it accumulates in each body. By the time the top predator eats its prey, it may as well be eating the poison rather than the prey.

Humans are clearly the top predator in our world. While we may or may not be physically ingesting the poisons we have released into Nature, we certainly receive them back on a spiritual and emotional level. This directly impacts our energy fields. It may even result in physical conditions that have no medically known cause.

As healers, we must be aware of the possibilities in this. This is a similar concept to the ancient shamanic belief that dirt or mud could cause skin problems or illnesses. The ancient shamans attributed this to spirits in these pieces of earth. In order for healing to take place, the earth had to be used to remove the illness and then be ritually returned to its place of origin.

Many modern people care nothing for maintaining local spirits or land. We would never return earth to its original place, even if it has been contaminated by our disease. Often that "disease" takes the form of environmental contaminants. We clean them up as best we can or truck out the offending dirt. We do not try to restore honor or respect to the Spirits of Place.

People also have a tendency to get so wrapped up in their own pain that they are unable to see beyond it. We can see this in the people who come to us for "healing." Some of us can waver between desperately wanting someone to fix it for us because it is way too serious for us to handle on our own, and simply resigning ourselves to the belief that whatever is plaguing us is obviously so deep and intense that it can never be cured.

A healer never wants to belittle the feelings of another person, but sometimes things need to be put in perspective. When viewed along with the destruction of the rainforest or the extinction of yet another entire species, is this condition honestly something that cannot be overcome? Perhaps and perhaps not, but it can be very freeing to see our problems from a much larger perspective.

For both the individual in need of some perspective and the one who is exhibiting symptoms that may be ecological in source, some form of active participation in Nature is extremely beneficial. Whether a simple reconnection is all that is needed, or whether an active stand in protecting the environment is called for, the healer needs to be aware of the healing effects of the world around us. The possibilities inherent in ecological therapy should be a part of every healer's toolkit.

Journey on this or ask questions that will assist you in determining if the person you are working for is alienated from Nature. To be honest, most modern people are disconnected to some extent. Try to determine if there is any fear or resistance associated with re-establishing a relationship with the natural world. If at all possible, you may want to do some of your healing or preliminary work in a natural setting.

If you determine that this is a contributing factor in the complaints, you need to find the best way to heal this rift. Taking someone out for a three-day vision quest is not going to solve all his or her problems. Certainly retreats of this type are valuable, but they require preliminary as well as considerable post-retreat work to fully integrate the visions and bring them into one's daily life. Even then, the insights of one retreat are not all-encompassing. There are certain to be other layers of concern or other issues that were not touched upon in this one session, even if it lasted a full week.

Pulitzer-prize–winning scientist and Harvard University professor E. O. Wilson coined the term *biophilia* to denote our innate and potentially genetic disposition to affiliate with other life forms. Its opposite has been termed *biophobia* and this is an equally valid concept.

When dealing with individuals who have a fear of or some resistance to wilderness interactions, the healer must proceed gradually and with caution. Moving forward too quickly is likely to have the same results as diving unprepared into soul retrieval with no ongoing support system. This tactic is likely to create additional blocks and fragmentation, while increasing the experience of biophobia.

It has also been suggested that, in the hopes of raising environmental awareness, we may actually be contributing to biophobia or desensitization through certain tactics. When people, particularly children, are faced with continual or extreme examples of ecological abuse, they recoil into self-protection and shut down in order to stop the pain. Victims of physical, emotional, and sexual abuse exhibit similar mechanisms.

Even when we are attempting to simply put things in perspective, it is a healer's responsibility to gently open the heart of the person in need to allow energy and feeling to flow and healing to occur. We never want to risk premature or forced emotional reactions because of the potentially damaging backlash. It is important to move along at the patient's pace, without being afraid of taking a step or two backward if necessary at times.

Edward C. Wolf wrote, "To arouse biophilia, science is not enough. Money, for all its power, is not enough. Culture—literature, drama, music, painting, filmmaking, the humble activity of learning itself—may be the way to engage the heart."[1] Indeed, as is evidenced throughout this book, experiential activities are the path to healing the heart and soul. If we have determined that a reconnection to the natural world is a necessary ingredient in a cure, then we are likely to be most effective when using art, song, journeying, and writing, combined with outdoor walks and exercises.

You may notice that most of the exercises in this book begin with a request for permission from the Land. In my tradition, prayers take four parts. First, we offer thanks to those beings that guide us and bless us. Then we offer prayers for others. Only then do we ask for blessings for ourselves. Finally, we give thanks again, praying that our every action be done in honor.

While it is part of the shamanic tradition to be in Nature with honor, a natural feeling of gratitude and respect often develops as our relationship to Nature grows. I have given very simple and relatively nonspiritual workshops to mainstream people on reconnecting with the Living Earth. Inevitably, these people find that they are drawn to thanking the plants and animals when we leave a place.

Requesting permission from the Land can make many people feel silly or embarrassed. We are not used to asking permission unless we

---

1. Wolf, "Arousing Biophilia."

are required to with authority figures. Many modern people only give thanks as a sort of payment when someone does something nice for us because we want to be seen as having "manners." Nature is under our control, so why would we ask permission or give it thanks?

My family makes it a practice to ask permission of the Spirits of Place whenever we enter a wild area. We honor the local spirits and we always give offerings of thanks when we leave. In this way, we enter into sacred relationship with the area. Every place becomes a sacred site and our energy is held at a higher level. As a result, we have had some surprising experiences of kinship and protection in the wild.

Even from a purely selfish, disconnected perspective, we need other living things to survive. At the most basic level, we need air to breathe and food to eat. The natural world provides these things and we honor all involved when we develop an attitude of gratitude. This attitude also tends to carry over into our interactions with the natural world, reducing pollution and increasing stewardship.

The following exercise is designed to allow this natural gratitude to develop. It is important that it be performed in a safe space, free from the potential for physical and emotional injury. This is something a healer may choose to guide individuals though for specific reasons. You might also consider involving several of those you are working with at any given time. Sometimes the group energy and the ability to share these experiences can contribute significantly to the healing at hand.

I have led groups through this exercise in various natural spaces. I find that after the first few minutes, they tend to get so involved in the experience that they forget about the other people around them. Even so, it is preferred that this be done in a relatively quiet place with a fair degree of privacy.

WALKING IN HONOR

Begin by asking this place and its beings to assist and guide you through this experience. Close your eyes and take a deep breath.

As you open your eyes, walk to the first thing your eyes rest on. Breathe deeply until you feel some sort of connection with this object. Feel how it must feel to be this object. Thank it for sharing this space with you and allow yourself to be led to whatever seems to call your attention next.

Continue to give thanks and move on to the next thing until you feel a change in your consciousness or a kinship with the place.

Thank this area for its guidance and for sharing its essence with you.

Note any insights or changes in your awareness that result from this exercise.

The Link to the Stars

It is commonly understood that the stuff of what we are made originated in ancient stars. The planets, the stars, and us—we are all created from the same matter that is continually recycled throughout the universe. We share our building blocks with All That Is. Therefore, we have the ability to resonate with the earth and the heavens, just as we can call upon cellular memories to reconnect with our heritage and ancestral lands.

Ancient peoples saw the hand of the Creator in all of Nature, from lightning and other weather to meteorites and the constellations. The sun and moon have always held a special place in native mythologies. Legends of ancestors that came from the starry heavens are prolific among indigenous cultures. Even certain animals are said to have arrived on earth from their homes among the stars.

We are not truly isolated from the rest of the solar system here within our Earth's atmosphere. Solar flares are known to affect and even interrupt radio communications here on Earth. Charged particles from the sun contact atmospheric molecules—primarily oxygen and nitrogen—and result in the aurora borealis, which has intrigued and frightened people for millennia.

The following journey is something that both healer and those in need may use for guidance and personal healing. It is detailed enough for the beginning journeyer, yet open enough to allow a true shamanic journey to develop. This journey has been used for guidance and divination, however, this journey is healing in itself.

SUN JOURNEY

You are flying up toward the sun. As you rise toward its center, you become aware of a smaller Sun in your own center. The closer you get, the more brightly your inner Sun shines. Your energy is resonating with that of the sun and you are drawn into its center to a specific area. Notice any other beings that are present. Be aware of how this area appears to you.

Ask that you might receive any guidance or healing that you need at this time. If there is a specific issue or question that is concerning you, ask for assistance with this. Become aware that your own inner Sun responds to life events, thought, and energetic environments. When you are experiencing dishonesty or an environment that is not beneficial to you, the light of this Sun diminishes. When you are living your own truth and in the presence of other people and situations that hold integrity, your Sun blazes forth with light.

Give thanks to this place and any beings that you encountered for their guidance and presence and return to your physical body.

Although seasonal affective disorder—basically a lack of sunlight—is the only condition accepted by the American Psychiatric Association as having an environmental source, many modern people still recognize the influence of the celestial bodies on our lives. Astrology has become so commonly used that it has found its way into the clichés of our culture: "What's your sign, baby?"

I have found astrology to be an incredible tool in a wide variety of ways. For the shamanic healer, we can use the energies and archetypes of the planets and their signs for both astrological insights into life situations and ailments as well as for truly powerful journeying. I find this to be particularly beneficial around the new and full moons and on any solar or lunar eclipses.

Then I enter the shamanic journey with the appropriate archetype or with an image of the astrological chart for the day in question. If I have a particular question or healing case in mind for this time period, I take that intent into the journey with me. These journeys can be truly profound and often give me much deeper insight into how the planetary placements will affect me or those I am working with at the time.

The journey outlined below is the basic outline I use for astrological journeying. Before entering the journey, choose a planet, constellation/zodiac sign, or a particular planetary transit for your focus. This will be your intended destination as you enter your shamanic trance.

ZODIAC JOURNEY

Begin your journey outside under the night sky. The moon is dark, allowing the light of stars to shine brightly overhead. Look around until you find your destination. You will know it as soon as you see it. Perhaps it shines more brightly or in a different color, or perhaps you simply feel a pull as your eyes pass over it. Give thanks for the presence of the stars and their light. Then ask for guidance with any specific question or issue you have in mind.

Allow the experience to unfold as it will, trusting that you will learn what you need to at this time. You may meet with a deity or animal representing the archetype or energy of your chosen stars. You may be drawn up to these stars or ride the starlight to another world. When you feel you have received what you will in this session, thank those present for their guidance and return to your physical body.

Even healers who do not follow astrological transits frequently work according to the phases of the moon. Full moon drumming and ritual groups abound in nearly every area I have visited throughout the United States. Fewer people seem to choose to hold special circles on new moons, but this is not uncommon. I used to work with a shamanic journeying group that gathered out in the wilderness whenever possible at the new moon.

The following journey is wonderful as a true journey or as a meditation to accompany a moon phase ritual. It is even more powerful when used in conjunction with a particular phase of the moon.

MOON JOURNEY

Begin your journey outside under the moon. Notice the phase of the moon. Is it full, dark, or crescent? Is it waning or waxing? Feel the light of the moon on your body as it begins to sink into your skin, filling your being. Give thanks for the presence of the moon and its energy. Then ask for guidance with your specific question or issue.

Allow the experience to unfold as it will, trusting that you will learn what you need to at this time. You may meet with a god or goddess of the moon. You may be drawn up to the moon itself or ride the moonbeams to another world. When you feel you have received what you will in this session, thank those present for their guidance and return to your physical body.

The phases of the moon were the basis for the first calendars and many native peoples still perceive time to be a circular phenomenon, which is very different from the modern linear construct. In the absence of the fluorescent lights and concrete of our modern world, most women will menstruate along with the phases of the moon. Even the tides of our vast oceans follow the moon. Throughout the ages, the actions of this heavenly body have been recognized for their impact on our world.

We can find healing among the heavens. In truth, we may find even greater balance through re-establishing our link to the stars while we develop our relationships to the earth. The multiverse is truly a macrocosm that reflects our own multidimensional existence.

Many people find that the Upperworlds are experienced as celestial or spacelike in nature. People have been known to visit other planets and get extraterrestrial guidance during Upperworld journeys. The Lowerworlds are often experienced as more earthlike, although the shamanic journey is highly variable and extremely personal. I have found that Upperworld experiences are often related to higher chakra activity. Lowerworld journeys are frequently triggered or accompanied by activity in the lower chakras that ground us into physical reality.

In reconnecting to both earth and heavens, healers balance the energy flowing through us as we stabilize chakras and the energy fields of those in need of healing. The EarthStar Meditation in chapter 2 is an excellent balancing tool for these energies. We can combine this meditation and shamanic journeying with art, music, and writing to further strengthen these connections for ourselves and those we are called to heal.

11

LIVING IN BALANCE

The ultimate goal of healing is to restore balance and re-establish a harmonious energy flow. However, the healing does not cease once that is done. This process does not cease once we become Healers. Healing is a lifelong process of learning, growth, and change. It is a dynamic state of being that we must each strive toward every day.

To guide those who come to us for healing in developing an understanding of this process is a large part of our responsibility as healers. Unlike Western medical practitioners, we do not simply turn people loose once they are restored to a functional state. Our highest goal is to heal and empower the individual so that together we can contribute to a healing and empowered society.

To live in balance does not guarantee the ideal life with no pain, no illness, and no challenges. It does not mean we are enlightened, superior beings with all the wisdom in the multiverse. I know some people who believe if someone knows a great deal about a spiritual path, magickal system, or religion, that they are an "advanced" person and therefore should be above the human experience.

First of all, knowledge and wisdom may well be mutually exclusive. A very young child may be exceptionally wise without knowing much about our world. Similarly, an individual who has amassed knowledge may be egocentric and lack both common sense and wisdom.

Knowledge has a way of limiting us without our awareness. It may preclude tolerance and understanding, eliminating true compassion and appreciation for diversity in all things. It is simply knowledge, nothing more and nothing less. Depending on how you handle it, this knowledge may create blocks to true wisdom, which flows through us from the multiverse. Wisdom is not something that we possess. It is not something to be stored in the memory centers of our brains.

In this book, I encourage the reader to gain education and knowledge of the methods you will use in your healing practice, but I implore you not to allow that to prevent you from exploring. Don't permit yourself to get overly comfortable in any plateau of learning or social status. Remember that there is always something more to learn. While you may be an accepted expert in one area, you do not know it all, not even about that particular area.

Living in balance is about awareness, about raising one's consciousness to the next level. When we strive to maintain balance in our lives, we recognize that getting to know ourselves and healing our own wounds is a lifelong journey and we consciously choose to embark upon it. While we practice discernment regarding friends and acquaintances, we do not denigrate other people.

We recognize that the actions and behaviors we prefer to eliminate from our lives are simply actions and behaviors. These do not tell us anything about the spirit behind the personality. These behaviors are frequently the result of pain and fear—and an individual that does not know how to move through this.

The Compassion Exercise below is a wonderful one to use frequently.[1] I recommend it for use by both healers and those with

---

1. ReSurfacing® workbook page 61, Avatar® materials by Harry Palmer. Excerpted with permission by Harry Palmer © 2000. Avatar® and ReSurfacing® are registered trademarks of Star's Edge, Inc.

whom they are working. We all get caught up in judgment or anger from time to time. This exercise can be done anywhere and it helps bring us back to a place of compassion and wisdom. In fact, I recommend that this exercise be done anywhere you find people, preferably strangers in the beginning.

COMPASSION EXERCISE

1. With attention on the person, repeat to yourself: "Just like me, this person is seeking some happiness for his/her life."
2. With attention on the person, repeat to yourself: "Just like me, this person is trying to avoid suffering in his/her life."
3. With attention on the person, repeat to yourself: "Just like me, this person has known sadness, loneliness, and despair."
4. With attention on the person, repeat to yourself: "Just like me, this person is seeking to fulfill his/her needs."
5. With attention on the person, repeat to yourself: "Just like me, this person is learning about life."

Variations
1. To be done by couples and family members to increase understanding of each other.
2. To be done on old enemies and antagonists still present in one's memories.

Many studies have shown that people with a spiritual connection to a Great Spirit and the natural world may heal more quickly and resist illness more effectively than other people. These studies have usually focused on the manifestation of this connection as prayer or meditation. There have been similar studies showing the powerful healing effects of prayer, even when the subjects were not aware that they were the focus of prayer.

Life has a way of interfering with one's spiritual connection through stress and fear. We get preoccupied or overworked and postpone our spiritual practice. Our energy becomes scattered and fixed or lost through auric injury and soul fragmentation. Part of living a healthy, balanced life is finding a way to maintain those spiritual connections. Even if you can only manage ten minutes each day to practice a breathing technique, sing your power song, or meditate on your spirit guides, this keeps the flow moving.

There was a time in my life when ten minutes was all I could manage. I did my breathing exercises in the bathroom at work because I was asleep by the time I sat down at home. Those few minutes were all I needed. I resisted illness when my coworkers were all sick. My stress levels were low and my energy was high. On the drive to and from work, I rarely listened to the radio, preferring to sing my power song or listen to a more spiritual tape instead.

The goal is not to stay "high" all the time and coast through life without getting involved in the experience. There are going to be times when what we really need is a good bottle of wine and some chocolate so we can feel better as we wallow in emotion for a little while. Yet we keep it all in balance and we reconnect with the natural world whenever we can.

Ethics of Healing

Throughout this book I have touched on the ethics inherent in the healing vocation, but this is important enough to warrant a section of its own. I chose to place it here at the end of this book in the chapter on living in balance. I did not want it to get lost in the large amount of information in the previous chapters, but more importantly, it speaks to who we are and how we live our daily lives, so it rightly belongs in this chapter.

Often we expect that ethics are simply assumed. They are common sense and everyone understands them. Yet we are all terribly surprised and upset when someone crosses the line and does something unethical. Many times those healers did not fully understand why their actions were unethical.

When we heal, we place the best interests of the person in need as our top priority. This does not mean that we negate our own needs or well-being, and we never place that at risk, but our every action is made in respect and honor. We never act in a way that might harm the patient on any level of being. In light of this, we need to keep this in mind and consider it carefully before taking any action.

It would be ideal if all healers took an oath, much like the modern Hippocratic-type oath taken by American medical students. Upon the taking of this oath, new doctors solemnly vow, by whatever they hold sacred, to live their lives and perform their practice in honor, avoid corruption and wrongdoing at all costs, work to the best of their ability for the good of their patients, and keep all that is said and done in private with a patient in the strictest confidence.

Each one of these items is of utmost importance. Certainly it is good business to encourage trust by maintaining confidentiality and develop our abilities in order to continue to attract clients, but for a true Healer it goes far beyond this. It may be perceived in an almost homeopathic way. Polluted water may help your crops to grow, until the pollutants reach a critical level, but you would not want to eat food grown in this way. Similarly, the healer whose total energy field resonates with respect and integrity is the one that will effect true and long-term healing.

Living an impeccable life is not easy. At times, we all want to sink into destructive habits. We may want to gossip about one session or complain about another. Sometimes we are just so tired that we would rather just stay home and lie on the couch, or something special comes up and we'd prefer to be there than heading off to a healing session. Everyone goes through it and there is no value in feeling guilty about it.

Yet we have committed to a very special path of service. We face our feelings and move through them, releasing them as we refocus on the work at hand and the blessings that have brought us to this point. We open to that higher power that flows through us as we heal and suddenly all those feelings dissolve into nothingness, leaving only the Healer remaining.

We will know peace and healing when we can truly and honestly connect with other beings, Nature, and our own inner selves. When we remember that we are integral and interconnected parts of All That Is, then we will forget loneliness, judgment, fear, and hatred. As Wounded Healers, we may become catalysts for change, respect, and integrity in our reality. We will no longer allow old and often indoctrinated stories to control us. Only then will we be able to live consciously and be fully present, not simply tolerating diversity, but celebrating it in harmony.

The path of the Healer is a complex one that involves considerable personal work in addition to the work we undertake on the behalf of others. It can be frustrating, painful, and sad at times. It is incredibly humbling and empowering at the same time. It is also a path filled with joy, blessings, and wonder. To be a Healer is to hold oneself to a high level of integrity and ethics. It is to give of one's time and energy in service to the community. It is to set aside egocentrism so that we may merge with something much greater than the individual identities we wear in this lifetime. If you are on this path, even if only to be of service to yourself or your own family, I honor you and thank you.

RHYTHM RESOURCES

African Rhythm Traders
drum building supplies: djembe and dunun
424 NE Broadway
Portland, OR 97232
phone: (800) 894-9149
fax: (503) 397-4343
information@rhythmtraders.com
http://www.rhythmtraders.com/

All One Tribe, Inc.
wide variety of finished drums
P.O. Drawer N
Taos, NM 87571
phone: (800) 442-DRUM, or (800) 442-3786
fax: (505) 751-0509
beat@allonetribe.org
http://www.allonetribedrum.com

Cedar River Drum Co.
cedar frame finished drums
219 7th St. NW
Mt. Vernon, IA 52314
phone: (319) 895-0774
sales@cedarriverdrumco.com
http://cedarriverdrumco.com/

Everyone's Drumming
wide selection of finished drums and supplies
P.O. Box 361
Putney, VT 05346
phone: (800) 326-0726
every1drm@sover.net
http://www.everyonesdrumming.com/

Full Circle Drums
doumbeks and djembeks plus supplies
36 San Marcos Trout Club
Santa Barbara, CA 93105
phone and fax: (805) 967-2541
http://www.fullcircledrums.com/

Grey Wolf
octagon-shaped frame drums: finished and kits
P.O. Box 711
Coquille, OR 97423
phone: (451) 396-2095 or (888) WOLF-DRUM
greywolf@greywolfdrums.com
http://www.harborside.com/~jalapeno/

Hobgoblin Music
Celtic and World drums plus many other instruments
920 State Highway 19
Red Wing, MN 55066
phone: (877) 866-3936 (1-US STONEYEND)
fax: (651) 388-8460
stoney@stoneyend.com
http://www.hobgoblin-usa.com/local/order.htm

Jo-an the DragonLady
ceramic drums
General Delivery
PineHill, NM 87357
phone: (505) 775-3083
drgndeer47@yahoo.com

Mid-East Mfg., Inc.
huge variety of finished instruments
7694 Progress Circle
W. Melbourne, FL 32904
phone: (800) 673-1517
info@mid-east.com
http://www.mid-east.com/

RECOMMENDED READING

General

Ajaya, Swami, Ph.D. *Psychotherapy East and West: A Unifying Paradigm.* Honesdale, Pa.: Himalayan International Institute of Yoga Science and Philosophy of the U.S.A., 1983.

Brennan, Barbara. *Hands of Light.* New York: Bantam Books, 1988.

Champe, Pamela C., and Richard A. Harvey, Ph.D. *Lippincott's Illustrated Reviews: Biochemistry.* Philadelphia, Pa.: Lippincott Williams & Wilkins Publishers, 1994.

Madden, Kristin. *Pagan Parenting.* St. Paul, Minn.: Llewellyn Publications, 2000.

———. *Shamanic Guide to Death and Dying.* St. Paul, Minn.: Llewellyn Publications, 1999.

Roszak, Theodore, Mary E. Gomes, and Allen D. Kanner, eds. *Ecopsychology: Restoring the Earth, Healing the Mind.* San Francisco: Sierra Club Books, 1995.

Tedeschi, Marc. *Essential Anatomy: For the Healing and Martial Arts.* Trumbull, Conn.: Weatherhill, 2000.

Zand, Janet, L.Ac., O.M.D., Rachel Walton, R.N., and Bob Rountree, M.D. *Smart Medicine for a Healthier Child.* New York: Avery Publishing Group, 1994.

Bodywork

Juhan, Deane, and Ken Dychtwald. *Job's Body: A Handbook for Bodywork.* Kingston, N.Y.: Barrytown Ltd., 1998.

McClure, Vimala Schneider. *Infant Massage.* New York: Bantam Books, 1989.

Namikoshi, Toru. *The Complete Book of Shiatsu Therapy.* Tokyo: Japan Publications, Inc., 1994.

Ya-li, Fan. *Chinese Pediatric Massage Therapy.* Boulder, Colo.: Blue Poppy Press, 1994.

Breathing

Farhi, Donna. *The Breathing Book: Good Health and Vitality Through Essential Breath Work.* New York: Henry Holt, 1996.

Rama, Swami, Rudolph Ballentine, M.D., and Alan Hymes, M.D. *Science of Breath.* Honesdale, Pa.: Himalayan International Institute of Yoga Science and Philosophy of the U.S.A., 1979.

Divination

Andrews, Ted. *Animal Speak.* St. Paul, Minn.: Llewellyn Publications, 1993.

Bunning, Joan. *Learning the Tarot: A Tarot Book for Beginners.* York Beach, Maine: Samuel Weiser, 1998.

Carr-Gomm, Philip and Stephanie. *Druid Animal Oracle.* New York: Simon & Schuster, 1995.

Rezendes, Paul. *Tracking and the Art of Seeing.* New York: HarperCollins, 1999.

Sams, Jamie, and David Carson. *Medicine Cards.* Santa Fe, N. Mex.: Bear & Co., 1988.

Tyson, Donald. *Scrying for Beginners.* St. Paul, Minn.: Llewellyn Publications, 1997.

Drum-making

Djembe-L FAQ. Vols. 8–9.
  http://www.drums.org/djembefaq/

Kristel, Dru. *Breath was the First Drummer.* Santa Fe, N. Mex.: QX Publications/A.D.A.M. Inc., 1995.

Healing Postures

Gore, Belinda. *Ecstatic Body Postures.* Santa Fe, N. Mex.: Bear & Co., 1995.

Singh, Ravi. *Kundalini Yoga for Strength, Success, & Spirit.* New York: White Lion Press, 1991.

Herbs

Brill, Steve, and Evelyn Dean. *Identifying and Harvesting Edible and Medicinal Plants in Wild (And Not So Wild) Places.* New York: Hearst Books, 1994.

Morrison, Dorothy. *Bud, Blossom & Leaf.* St. Paul, Minn.: Llewellyn Publications, 2001.

Santillo, Humbart. *Natural Healing with Herbs.* Prescott, Ariz.: Hohm Press, 1984.

Swerdlow, Joel L. *Nature's Medicine.* Washington, D.C.: National Geographic Society, 2000.

Homeopathy

Boericke, William, M.D. *Pocket Manual of Homeopathic Materia Medica and Repertory.* New Delhi, India: B. Jain Publishers, 1995.

Panos, Maesimund B., M.D., and Jane Heimlich. *Homeopathic Medicine at Home.* New York: Jeremy P. Tarcher, Inc., 1980.

Nutrition

Balch, James F., M.D., and Phyllis A. Balch, C.N.C. *Prescription for Nutritional Healing.* New York: Avery Penguin Putnam, 2000.

Pitchford, Paul. *Healing with Whole Foods: Oriental Traditions and Modern Nutrition.* Berkeley, Calif.: North Atlantic Books, 1993.

Spellwork

Buckland, Raymond. *Practical Candleburning Rituals.* St. Paul, Minn.: Llewellyn Publications, 1987.

Malbrough, Ray T. *Charms, Spells, and Formulas.* St. Paul, Minn.: Llewellyn Publications, 1986.

GLOSSARY

Aborigines—Indigenous tribal people of Australia.

animal ally—Spirit guide in animal form.

Awen—Divine inspiration; also known as *imbas* to the Welsh.

Bard—The keepers of the verbal traditions of the Celtic peoples. Simply put, these are the poets, musicians, and storytellers.

Bhramari—A pranayama (breathing) exercise. From the Sanskrit word for "bumble bee."

bodywork—Any of a wide variety of healing techniques involving manipulation of the physical body. This includes massage, acupuncture, Rolfing, and so on.

body soul—That part of one's spirit that is bound to the physical body. It animates and maintains the life of the physical body while the free soul travels.

Brighid—Celtic goddess of healing, poetry, and smithcraft, midwifery, and fire.

Celts—Originally Indo-European people, commonly regarded as native to the British Isles.

chakras—Energy vortexes at the conjunction points of the human physical and energy bodies.

Crane Bag—*See also* Medicine pouch. The Crane Bag is the Celtic version of the Medicine pouch. Its origins probably lie with Mannanan, the sea god who kept his most precious items in a bag made of the skin of the crane.

divination—Any of a wide variety of methods designed to gain access to knowledge that is not readily available in everyday life. This may include gaining deep insight into situations, telling the future, or diagnosing illness without medical testing.

Dreaming—An Australian aboriginal word meaning the collective unconscious.

Dreamtime—In the Australian aboriginal belief, the time before creation of the physical world.

druids—The elite ritualists, scholars, healers, diplomats, and shamans of the Celts.

free soul—The astral or dreaming body. A body of energy that is part of the individual spirit but is free to travel without the body. Also called the *spirit double* or *energy body.*

healing matrix—A tool for energetic healing developed by West Hardin.

homeopathy—A therapeutic medical system that treats conditions using minute amounts of specific remedies that would induce the patient's same symptoms in a normal, healthy person.

initiation—The experiential process by which an individual becomes a shaman.

Lowerworld—The shamanic realm that is generally perceived to be lower in space than our present reality. It is often associated with the ancestors, animal guides, and the Earth.

Medicine pouch—A bag or pouch containing sacred objects that hold or represent the bearer's Medicine: spirit allies and personal power. It may be seen as a small and private portable altar.

Middleworld—The shamanic realm that we occupy during normal consciousness.

mudra—Hand positions that induce altered states of consciousness and/or affect the flow of energy through the body; ecstatic postures or yoga forms for the hands only.

multiverse—The shamanic view of the cosmos, combining the interrelated multiple dimensions, or Otherworlds.

nagual—Awareness and being beyond the ordinary; that which is beyond reason and analysis.

Rescue Remedy—One of the Bach Flower Remedies that is particularly effective for any type of trauma or fright.

Saami—Indigenous people of northern Sweden, Norway, Finland, and northwest Russia; more commonly known by the derogatory terms *Lapps* or *Laplanders.*

scrying—A form of divination involving a focal point, such as water, oil, or clouds, that stimulates psychic sight.

shamanizing—Performing the work of the shaman.

shapeshifting—The ability to change the shape of the physical or energy body. This is often associated with a merging of animal guide and shaman.

soul fragment—A part of the spirit that has been splintered or broken off from the whole, generally due to trauma.

spirit guide—A spirit being that acts as guardian, teacher, and guide in the physical realm and the Otherworlds.

string theory—A field of modern physics that proposes that tiny, one-dimensional loops, termed *strings,* exist within subatomic particles. The vibrations of these strings result in a universe made up of eleven dimensions.

Upperworld—The shamanic realm that is generally perceived to be higher in space than our present reality. It is often associated with humanoid guides and clairvoyance.

yoga—A psychophysical practice, which was developed in India and has roots going back five thousand years. The word *yoga* means "union."

REFERENCES

Ajaya, Swami, Ph.D. *Psychotherapy East and West: A Unifying Paradigm.* Honesdale, Pa.: Himalayan International Institute of Yoga Science and Philosophy of the U.S.A., 1983.

Arkani-Hamed, N., S. Dimopoulos, and G. Dvali. "The Universe's Unseen Dimensions." *Scientific American* 283, no. 2 (2000): 62–69.

Brennan, Barbara. *Hands of Light.* New York: Bantam Books, 1988.

Conway, D. J., and Lisa Hunt. *The Celtic Dragon Tarot.* St. Paul, Minn.: Llewellyn Publications, 1999.

Flanagan, Patrick, M.D., and Gael Crystal Flanagan, M.D. "Biophilia & Emotional Well-Being." N.p.: 1999.

Gilbert, William H. *The Eastern Cherokees.* Smithsonian Institution, Bureau of American Ethnology Bulletin 133. Washington, D.C., 1943.

Gore, Belinda. *Ecstatic Body Postures: An Alternate Reality Workbook.* Santa Fe, N. Mex.: Bear & Company, 1995.

Greene, Brian. *The Elegant Universe.* New York: Vintage Books, 1999.

"Hippocratic Oath." Microsoft® Encarta® Online Encyclopedia 2000. http://encarta.msn.com © 1997–2000 Microsoft Corporation. All rights reserved.

Hull, Arthur. *Drum Circle Spirit: Facilitating Human Potential through Rhythm.* Tempe, Ariz.: White Cliffs Media, Inc., 1998.

Madden, Kristin. *Pagan Parenting.* St. Paul, Minn.: Llewellyn Publications, 2000.

———. *Shamanic Guide to Death and Dying*. St. Paul, Minn.: Llewellyn Publications, 1999.

Matthews, Caitlin and John. *The Encyclopaedia of Celtic Wisdom*. Element Books: Dorset, England.

Mooney, James. "Cherokee Theory and Practice of Medicine." *Journal of American Folklore* 3 (1890): 44–50.

Mooney, James, and Frans M. Olbrechts, eds. *The Swimmer Manuscript: Cherokee Sacred Formulas and Medicinal Prescriptions*. Smithsonian Institution, Bureau of American Ethnology Bulletin 99. Washington, D.C., 1932.

"Piezoelectric Effect." Microsoft® Encarta® Online Encyclopedia 2001. http://encarta.msn.com © 1997–2001 Microsoft Corporation. All rights reserved.

Rama, Swami, Rudolph Ballentine, M.D., and Alan Hymes, M.D. *Science of Breath*. Honesdale, Pa.: Himalayan International Institute of Yoga Science and Philosophy of the U.S.A., 1979.

Redmond, Layne. *When the Drummers Were Women: A Spiritual History of Rhythm*. New York: Three Rivers Press, 1997.

Roszak, Theodore, Mary E. Gomes, and Allen D. Kanner, eds. *Ecopsychology: Restoring the Earth, Healing the Mind*. San Francisco, Calif.: Sierra Club Books, 1995.

Rydving, Håkan. *The End of Drum-Time: Religious Change among the Lule Saami, 1670s–1740s*. Stockholm, Sweden: Norstedts Tryckeri, 1995.

Sanchez, Victor. *The Teachings of Don Carlos*. Santa Fe, N. Mex.: Bear & Company, 1995.

Wolf, Edward C. "Arousing Biophilia." 1989. http://arts.envirolink.org/interviews_and_conversations/EOWilson.html (Originally published in *Orion: People and Nature,* Summer 1989.)

INDEX

LLEWELLYN ORDERING INFORMATION

Order Online:
Visit our website at www.llewellyn.com, select your books, and order them on our secure server.

Order by Phone:
- Call toll-free within the U.S. at 1-877-NEW-WRLD (1-877-639-9753). Call toll-free within Canada at 1-866-NEW-WRLD (1-866-639-9753)
- We accept VISA, MasterCard, and American Express

Order by Mail:
Send the full price of your order (MN residents add 7% sales tax) in U.S. funds, plus postage & handling to:

Llewellyn Worldwide
2143 Wooddale Drive, Dept. 0-7387-0271-4
Woodbury, Minnesota 55125-2989, U.S.A.

Postage & Handling:
Standard (U.S., Mexico, & Canada). If your order is:
  $49.99 and under, add $3.00
  $50.00 and over, FREE STANDARD SHIPPING

AK, HI, PR: $15.00 for one book plus $1.00 for each additional book.

International Orders (airmail only):
  $16.00 for one book plus $3.00 for each additional book

Orders are processed within 2 business days.
Please allow for normal shipping time. Postage and handling rates subject to change.

How to Meet & Work
with Spirit Guides

TED ANDREWS

We often experience spirit contact in our lives but fail to recognize it for what it is. Now you can learn to access and attune to beings such as guardian angels, nature spirits and elementals, spirit totems, archangels, gods and goddesses—as well as family and friends after their physical death.

Contact with higher soul energies strengthens the will and enlightens the mind. Through a series of simple exercises, you can safely and gradually increase your awareness of spirits and your ability to identify them. You will learn to develop an intentional and directed contact with any number of spirit beings. Discover meditations to open up your subconscious. Learn which acupressure points effectively stimulate your intuitive faculties. Find out how to form a group for spirit work, use crystal balls, perform automatic writing, attune your aura for spirit contact, use sigils to contact the great archangels, and much more! Read *How to Meet and Work with Spirit Guides* and take your first steps through the corridors of life beyond the physical.

0-87542-008-7

192 pp., mass market $5.99

The Healer's Manual

A Beginner's Guide to Energy Therapies

TED ANDREWS

Did you know that a certain Mozart symphony can ease digestion problems . . . that swelling often indicates being stuck in outworn patterns . . . that breathing pink is good for skin conditions and loneliness? Most dis-ease stems from a metaphysical base. While we are constantly being exposed to viruses and bacteria, it is our unbalanced or blocked emotions, attitudes, and thoughts that deplete our natural physical energies and make us more susceptible to "catching a cold" or manifesting some other physical problem.

Healing, as approached in *The Healer's Manual,* involves locating and removing energy blockages wherever they occur—physical or otherwise. This book is an easy guide to simple vibrational healing therapies that anyone can learn to apply to restore homeostasis to their body's energy system. By employing sound, color, fragrance, etheric touch, and flower/gem elixirs, you can participate actively within the healing of your body and the opening of higher perceptions. You will discover that you can heal more aspects of your life than you ever thought possible.

0-87542-007-9
256 pp., 6 x 9, illus. $12.95

To order, call 1-877-NEW-WRLD
Prices subject to change without notice

Animal Speak

The Spiritual & Magical Powers of Creatures Great & Small

TED ANDREWS

The animal world has much to teach us. Some are experts at survival and adaptation, some never get cancer, some embody strength and courage, while others exude playfulness. Animals remind us of the potential we can unfold, but before we can learn from them, we must first be able to speak with them.

In this book, myth and fact are combined in a manner that will teach you how to speak and understand the language of the animals in your life. *Animal Speak* helps you meet and work with animals as totems and spirits—by learning the language of their behaviors within the physical world. It provides techniques for reading signs and omens in nature so you can open to higher perceptions and even prophecy. It reveals the hidden, mythical, and realistic roles of 45 animals, 60 birds, 8 insects, and 6 reptiles.

Animals will become a part of you, revealing to you the majesty and divine in all life. They will restore your childlike wonder of the world and strengthen your belief in magic, dreams, and possibilities.

0-87542-028-1
400 pp., 7 x 10, illus., photos $19.95

In the Shadow of the Shaman

Connecting with Self, Nature & Spirit

AMBER WOLFE

Presented in what the author calls a "cookbook shamanism" style, this book shares recipes, ingredients, and methods of preparation for experiencing some very ancient wisdoms: wisdoms of Native American and Wiccan traditions, as well as contributions from other philosophies of Nature as they are used in the shamanic way. Wheels, the circle, totems, shields, directions, divinations, spells, care of sacred tools, and meditations are all discussed. Wolfe encourages us to feel confident and free to use her methods to cook up something new, completely on our own. This blending of ancient formulas and personal methods represents what Ms. Wolfe calls Aquarian Shamanism.

In the Shadow of the Shaman is designed to communicate in the most practical, direct ways possible, so that the wisdom and the energy may be shared for the benefits of all. Whatever your system or tradition, you will find this to be a valuable book, a resource, a friend, a gentle guide, and support on your journey. Dancing in the shadow of the shaman, you will find new dimensions of Spirit.

0-87542-888-6
384 pp., 6 x 9, illus. $14.95

Bud, Blossom, & Leaf
The Magical Herb Gardener's Handbook

DOROTHY MORRISON

Now, in one single volume, is everything you need to know about herbs, both the mundane and the magical. Do you want to know how to tend them with hydroponic magic? Use them to clean your home? Or brew them into fine wines fit for the gods? This book not only answers these questions, but takes you on a magical journey down the garden path. Explore theme gardens and shapes to find the one that fits your magical purpose. Learn how to appease the home spirits so your garden will prosper and thrive. Travel outdoors and discover how to balance your garden into its magical best. Then step into the kitchen and whip up soothing ointments, beauty treatments, culinary delights, pest control solutions, and housecleaning supplies.

Packed with 125 spells, invocations, rituals, and recipes, *Bud, Blossom & Leaf* guides you on the path to becoming a magical herb gardener:

- Learn how to predict the weather and choose the best time frames for the gardening process
- Explore magical garden themes, garden shapes, and planting ideas
- Plant and grow a magical herb garden indoors or out
- Try out recipes for culinary, cosmetic, and first-aid uses

1-56718-443-X
192 pp., 7½ x 9⅛, illus. $14.95

To order, call 1-877-NEW-WRLD
Prices subject to change without notice

The Celtic Dragon Tarot

D. J. CONWAY AND LISA HUNT

Are dragons real? Since they do not live on the physical plane, scientists cannot trap and dissect them. Yet magicians and psychics who have explored the astral realms know firsthand that dragons do indeed exist, and that they make very powerful co-magicians. Dragons tap into deeper currents of elemental energies than humans. Because of their ancient wisdom, dragons are valuable contacts to call upon when performing any type of divination, such as the laying out of tarot cards. Tarot decks and other divination tools seem to fascinate them. *The Celtic Dragon Tarot* is the first deck to use the potent energies of dragons for divination, magickal spell working, and meditation.

Ancient mapmakers noted every unknown territory with the phrase "Here be dragons." Both tarot and magick have many uncharted areas. Not only will you discover dragons waiting there, but you will also find them to be extremely helpful when you give them the chance.

1-56718-182-1
Boxed set: 78 full-color cards with 216-pp., 6 x 9 book $29.95

To order, call 1-877-NEW-WRLD
Prices subject to change without notice

Charms, Spells & Formulas

For the Making and Use of Gris Gris Bags, Herb Candles, Doll Magick, Incenses, Oils and Powders

RAY MALBROUGH

Hoodoo magick is a blend of European techniques and the magick brought to the New World by slaves from Africa. Now you can learn the methods which have been used successfully by Hoodoo practitioners for nearly 200 years.

By using the simple materials available in nature, you can bring about the necessary changes to greatly benefit your life and that of your friends. You are given detailed instructions for making and using the *gris-gris* (charm) bags only casually or mysteriously mentioned by other writers. Malbrough not only shows how to make gris-gris bags for health, money, luck, love, and protection from evil and harm, but he also explains how these charms work. He also takes you into the world of doll magick to gain love, success, or prosperity. Complete instructions are given for making the dolls and setting up the ritual.

0-87542-501-1
192 pp., 5¼ x 8, illus. $7.95

Spanish edition:
Hechizos y conjuros
1-56718-455-3 $6.95

To order, call 1-877-NEW-WRLD
Prices subject to change without notice